MW01482719

Pocket Prayer Book
for Orthodox Christians

Containing:
Daily and Particular Prayers
Together with
The Ordinary of Saint Tikhon

First Edition, 2025

St. Tikhon of Moscow, Bishop & Confessor

Collect. O Lord God of the nations, who for the defense of the Orthodox Faith didst raise up and strengthen blessed Saint Tikhon, thy Bishop and Confessor, with great courage and self-denial: mercifully grant; that, by his example and intercessions, the hearts of the erring may be turned to the wisdom of the just, and the faithful may ever persevere in confession of thy true religion. Through Jesus Christ, Thy Son, Our Lord, who with Thee and the unity of the Holy Ghost, liveth and reineth, One God, world without end. Amen.

TO THOSE WHO HAVE CONTRIBUTED TO
THE WESTERN RITE OF THE
ANTIOCHIAN ORTHODOX CHRISTIAN
ARCHDIOCESE OF NORTH AMERICA

PREFACE

The Pocket Prayer Book of the Antiochian Orthodox Christian Archdiocese of North America inspired this book. We hope this book increases regular prayers in the faithful the way the original has for so many.

The editors have attempted to offer the prayers of the Western Rite. As a pocket prayer book, it is a partial offering of the prayers available, including only those prayers necessary to always have in your pocket.

This book was designed with busy people in mind, working at both mental and manual labor.

After several years of working on this project, we thank Julian Roberts for bringing this project to fruition.

We also express gratitude to His Grace Bishop John, the Very Rev. Edward Hughes, and the Very Rev. John Fenton.

This book is published through print-on-demand, which means it is easy to update. If you would like to submit errors and omissions, please send an email to press@stacollege.org.

TABLE OF CONTENTS

Part 1

Daily & Various Prayers

Prayers to Memorize

THE LORD'S PRAYER: Our Father who art in heaven, hallowed be thy name. Thy kingdom come. Thy will be done on earth as it is in heaven. Give us this day our daily bread, and forgive us our trespasses, as we forgive those who trespass against us, and lead us not into temptation, but deliver us from evil. Amen.

THE HAIL MARY: Hail, Mary, full of grace, the Lord is with thee. Blessed art thou amongst women and blessed is the fruit of thy womb, Jesus. Holy Mary, Mother of God, pray for us sinners, now and at the hour of our death. Amen.

THE APOSTLE'S CREED: I believe in God the Father Almighty, Maker of heaven and earth. And in Jesus Christ His only Son our Lord; Who was conceived by the Holy Ghost, born of the Virgin Mary; suffered under Pontius Pilate, was crucified, dead and buried; He descended into hell; the third day He rose again from the dead; He ascended into heaven, and sitteth on the right hand of God the Father Almighty; from thence He shall come to judge the quick and the dead. I believe in the Holy Ghost; the Holy Catholic Church; the communion of saints; the forgiveness of sins; the resurrection of the body, and the life everlasting. Amen.

MORNING PRAYERS

I praise Thee, O God, this day: I give myself unto Thee, O God, this day: I ask Thee, O God, to help me this day. Amen.

In the name of the Father, and of the Son, and of the Holy Ghost. Amen.

Come Holy Ghost, and fill the hearts of Thy faithful, and kindle in them the fire of Thy love.

Most holy and adorable Trinity, one God in three Persons, I believe that Thou art here present; I adore Thee with the deepest humility, and render to Thee, with my whole heart, the homage which is due to Thy sovereign majesty.

O my God, I most humbly thank Thee for all the favours Thou hast bestowed upon me up until this present moment. I give unto Thee hearty thanks that Thou hast created me after Thine own image and likeness, that Thou hast redeemed me by the precious Blood of Thy dear Son, and that Thou hast preserved me and brought me safe to the beginning of this another day. I offer unto Thee, O Lord, my whole being, and in particular all my thoughts, words, actions, and sufferings of this day. I consecrate them all to the glory of Thy name, beseeching Thee that through Thy grace and loving-kindness they may be found an acceptable offering in Thy sight.

Lord Jesus Christ, my Saviour and Master most adorable, model of all perfection, I resolve and will endeavor this day to imitate Thine example, striving to be like unto Thee, in mildness, humility, chastity, zeal, charity, and humble obedience and resignation. I will redouble my efforts that I may not fall this day into any of those sins which I have heretofore committed (name any besetting sin), and which I detest from the bottom of my heart and sincerely desire to forsake.

Thou, O Lord, who knowest my poverty and weakness, and that I am unable to do anything good without Thee, dost also know the duties, that lie before me this day, the dangers that may confront me this day and the sins that most beset me: deny me not, O God, the help of Thy grace and Thy protection; give me strength to avoid everything evil; and enable me to bear patiently all the trials and temptations which await me. Amen.

Our Father...Hail, Mary...I believe in God...

MID-DAY PRAYERS

The Angelus

Throughout the year, except for Paschaltide.
℣. The Angel of the Lord declared unto Mary:
℟. And she conceived by the Holy Ghost.
Hail, Mary...

℣. Behold the handmaid of the Lord:

℟. Be it unto me according to thy word. Hail, Mary...

℣. And the Word was made flesh:

℟. And dwelt among us. Hail, Mary...

℣. Pray for us, O holy Mother of God.

℟. That we may be made worthy of the promises of Christ.

Let us pray. Pour forth, we beseech Thee, O Lord, Thy grace into our hearts; that as we have known the Incarnation of Christ Thy Son by the message of an Angel, so, by His Passion and Cross, we may be brought to the glory of His Resurrection; through the same Jesus Christ our Lord. Amen.

The Regina Cæli

In Paschaltide, always said standing.

O Queen of heaven, rejoice! Alleluia.

For He whom so meetly thou barest, Alleluia,

Hath arisen, as He said, Alleluia.

Pray for us to God, Alleluia.

℣. Rejoice and be glad, O Virgin Mary. Alleluia.

℟. For the Lord hath risen indeed. Alleluia.

Let us pray. O God, who through the Resurrection of Thy Son our Lord Jesus Christ, didst vouchsafe to fill the world with joy; grant, we beseech Thee, that, through His Virgin Mother, Mary, we may lay hold on the joys of everlasting life. Through the same Jesus Christ our Lord. Amen.

EVENING PRAYERS

In the name of the Father, and of the Son and of the Holy Ghost. Amen.

Come Holy Ghost, and fill the hearts of Thy faithful, and kindle in them the fire of Thy love. O my God, I present myself before Thee at the end of another day, to offer Thee anew the homage of my heart humbly adore Thee, my Creator, my Redeemer, and my Judge.

Enable me, O Thy God, to return Thee thanks as I ought for all Thine inestimable blessings and favors. Thou hast thought of me, and loved me from all eternity; Thou hast formed me out of nothing; Thou hast delivered up Thy beloved Son to the ignominious death of the Cross for my redemption; Thou hast made me a member of Thy holy Church; Thou hast preserved me from falling into the abyss of eternal misery, when my sins had provoked Thee to punish me; and Thou hast graciously continued to spare me, even though I have not ceased to offend Thee. What return, O my God, can I make for Thine innumerable blessings, and particularly for the favors of this day? O ye Angels and Saints, unite with me in praising the God of mercies, who is so bountiful to so unworthy a creature.

Our Father...Hail, Mary...I believe in God...

O my God, sovereign Judge of men, who desirest not the death of a sinner, but that he should be converted and saved, enlighten my heart and mind, that I may know the sins which I have this day committed in thought, word, or deed, and give me the grace of true contrition.

Have I prayed? Have I wasted time? Have I judged? Have I engaged in gossip? Have I been dishonest, vain, or prideful? Have I been impatient, greedy, or indulged in bad thoughts? Have I used any bad words, been selfish in anything? Tell God today's sins, and then say:

O my God, I heartily repent, and am grieved that I have offended Thee, Who art so good: I humbly ask of Thee mercy and pardon; for the sake of Thy most beloved Son, Jesus Christ our Lord. I resolve, by the assistance of Thy grace, to amend my life and endeavor nevermore to offend Thee.

I confess to almighty God, to Blessed Mary ever Virgin, to blessed Michael: the Archangel, to blessed John the Baptist, to the holy Apostles Peter and Paul, and to all the Saints, that I have sinned exceedingly in thought, word, and deed, through my fault, through my fault, through my most grievous fault, and especially have I sinned this day in. . . (here repent of the sins committed during this day, remembering them each specifically) I beg Blessed Mary ever Virgin

13

blessed Michael the Archangel blessed John the Baptist, the holy Apostles Peter and Paul, and all the Saints to pray to the Lord our God for me.

May almighty God have mercy on me, forgive me my sins and bring me to everlasting life. Amen.

May the almighty and merciful Lord grant me pardon, absolution and remission of my sins. Amen.

BEDTIME PRAYERS

(kneel) In the name of the Father, and of the Son, and of the Holy Ghost. Amen.

Our Father...Hail, Mary...

I believe in God the Father Almighty, Maker of heaven and earth. And in Jesus Christ His only Son our Lord; Who was conceived by the Holy Ghost, born of the Virgin Mary; suffered under Pontius Pilate, was crucified, dead and buried; He descended into hell; the third day He rose again from the dead; He ascended into heaven, and sitteth on the right hand of God the Father Almighty; from thence He shall come to judge the quick and the dead. I believe in the Holy Ghost; the Holy Catholic Church; the communion of saints; the forgiveness of sins; the resurrection of the body, and the life everlasting. Amen.

I will lay me down in peace and take my rest, for it is Thou, Lord, only, that makest me dwell in safety. Visit, I beseech Thee, O Lord, this dwelling and drive far from it all snares of the enemy; let Thy holy Angels dwell herein, who may keep us in peace, and let Thy blessing be always upon us. Through Jesus Christ our Lord. Amen.

Lighten our darkness, we beseech Thee, O Lord: and by Thy great mercy defend us from all perils and dangers of this night, for the love of Thy only Son, our Saviour Jesus Christ. Amen.

Into Thy hands, O Lord, I commend my spirit, for Thou hast redeemed me, O Lord, Thou God of truth. Amen.

VARIOUS PRAYERS FOR OTHERS

In Any Tribulation

O almighty God, despise not Thy people who cry unto Thee in their affliction; but, for the glory of Thy name, turn away Thine anger, and help us in our tribulations.

Grace Before Meals

Bless us, O Lord, and these Thy gifts, which we are about to receive from Thy bounty, through Christ our Lord. Amen.

Thanksgiving After Meals

We give Thee thanks, O Almighty God, for all Thy mercies. Who livest and reignest, world without end. Amen.

For our Friends

O God, who, by the grace of the Holy Ghost, has poured into the hearts of Thy faithful the gifts of charity: grant to Thy servants and handmaids, for whom we implore Thy mercy, health both of body and soul; that they may love Thee with all their strength, and cheerfully perform those things which are pleasing unto Thee.

For a Husband or Wife

O Almighty God, who in the beginning didst institute the Sacrament of Marriage, bless with happiness our union, and grant that amid all the changes and chances of this mortal life, we may so live together in Thy love and fear, that in the end we may meet in Thy eternal home. Through Jesus Christ our Lord. Amen.

A Parent's Prayer

O Heavenly Father, I commend the soul(s) of my children (names) to Thee. Be Thou their God and Father; and mercifully supply whatever is wanting in me through frailty or negligence. Strengthen them to overcome the corruptions of the world, to resist all solicitations to evil, whether from within or without; and deliver them from the secret snares of the enemy. Pour Thy grace into their heart(s), and confirm and multiply in them the gifts of Thy Holy Ghost, that they may daily grow in grace and in knowledge of our Lord Jesus Christ; and so faithfully serving Thee here, may come to rejoice in Thy presence hereafter. Through the same Christ our Lord. Amen.

For those on a Journey

O God, who didst bring our fathers through the Sea, and bear them through the great waters singing praises unto Thy name: we humbly beseech Thee to vouchsafe to turn away all adversities from Thy servants during their journey, and to bring them with a calm voyage unto the haven where they would be.

For the Parish

Almighty and Everlasting God, who dost govern all things in heaven and earth, mercifully hear the supplications of us Thy servants, and grant unto this parish all things that are needful for its spiritual welfare; enlighten and guide its Priest(s); strengthen and increase the faithful; visit and relieve the sick; turn and soften the wicked; rouse the careless; recover the fallen; restore the penitent; remove all hindrances to the advancement of Thy truth; bring all to be of one heart and mind within the fold of Thy holy Church; to the honour and glory of Thy Name. Through Jesus Christ our Lord. Amen.

For Missions

O Great Lord of the harvest, send forth, we beseech Thee, labourers into the harvest of the world, that the grain which is even now ripe may not fall and perish through our neglect. Pour forth Thy sanctifying Ghost on Thy faithful people, and Thy converting grace on the heathen. Raise up, we pray Thee, a devout ministry among the native believers, that, all Thy people being knit together in one body in love, Thy holy Church may grow up into the measure of the stature of the fulness of Christ. Through Him Who died and rose for us all, the same Jesus Christ our Lord. Amen.

For the Increase of Religious Vocations

O Lord and lover of souls, pour out, we beseech Thee, upon Thy Church, the. spirit of religious vocation; and grant that those whom Thou dost call to give themselves to Thee in holy religion may have strength to resist all temptations, and remaining faithful to Thee in this life, may obtain Thy eternal rewards in the world to come. Through Jesus Christ our Lord. Amen.

For Monasteries and Convents

O Lord Jesus Christ, who saidst: Whoso loseth his life for My sake shall find it: Bestow, we pray Thee, Thine abundant blessing on those who have left all that they

18

may give themselves to this service, and grant that those whom Thou dost call may hear and obey Thy voice, and receive the manifold reward which Thou hast promised in this time, and in the world to come eternal life. Who livest and reignest, God, world without end. Amen.

For a Bishop

Grant, we beseech Thee, O Lord, to Thy servant our Bishop, that, by preaching and doing such things as are right, he may by the example of good works edify the minds of those under his authority, and receive of Thee, most tender Shepherd, an everlasting recompense and reward.

For a Priest

Jesus, eternal Priest, keep this thy Priest, Father (name), within the shelter of Thy Sacred Heart, where none may touch him. Keep unstained his anointed hands, which daily touch Thy sacred Body; keep unsullied his lips, purpled with Thy precious Blood; keep pure and unearthly his heart, sealed with sublime marks of Thy glorious priesthood. Let Thy holy love surround him, and keep him ever spotless from the world. Bless his labours with abundant fruit, and may they to whom he has ministered be here below his joy and consolation, and in heaven his beautiful and everlasting crown. Amen.

For the Dying

O Gracious Lord Jesus, who didst vouchsafe to die upon the Cross for us; Remember, we beseech Thee, all sick and dying persons, and grant that they may omit nothing which is necessary to make their peace with Thee before they die. Deliver them, O Lord, from the malice of the devil, and from all sin and evil, and grant them a happy end, for Thy loving mercy's sake. Amen.

For the Dead

O God, the Creator and Redeemer of all the faithful; grant unto the souls of Thy servants and handmaids the remission of all their sins; that through devout supplications they may obtain the pardon they have always desired. Who livest and reignest, God, world without end. Amen.

VARIOUS PRAYERS FOR ONESELF

From the Sarum Primer

God be in my head, and in my understanding;
God be in my eyes, and in my looking;
God be in my mouth, and in my speaking; God be in my heart, and in my thinking; God be at my end, and at my departing.

Prayer to One's Guardian Angel

Angel of God, my guardian dear, To whom His love commits me here, Ever this day be at my side, To light and guard, to rule and guide. Amen.

A Short Recommendation to God

Into the hands of Thy unspeakable mercy, O Lord, I recommend my soul and body; my senses, my words, my thoughts, and all my actions, with all the necessities of my body and soul; my going forth and my coming in; my faith and conversation; the course and end of my life; the day and the hour of my death; my rest and resurrection with the Saints and Elect.

Prayer to our Patron Saint

O great Saint, whose name I am privileged to bear, beneath whose special protection God has confided the care of my salvation, when at baptism I was adopted and made a child of God; do thou help me by thy continual intercession to lead a truly Christian life, and assist me, o Gracious protector of my soul, to recover and preserve the grace of baptism I may have lost by sin. Plead for me before God that I may receive the grace of following faithfully thy holy example and being protected by thee both throughout the length of this troublous life and at the hour of my death, I may rejoice with thee in glory everlasting. Amen.

On Going Out in the Morning

Show me, O Lord, Thy ways, and teach me Thy paths. Direct my steps according to Thy word, that no injustice may rule over me. Make perfect my walking in Thy paths, that my footsteps may not be moved. Jesus and Mary, we pray, be with us on our way.

On Going into Church

O Lord, in the multitude of Thy mercies, I will enter into Thy house, and worship Thee in Thy holy temple, and praise Thy name.

At Taking Holy Water

Sprinkle me, O Lord, with hyssop, and I shall be cleansed; wash me, and I shall be made whiter than snow. Create in me a clean heart, O God, and renew a right spirit within me.

Before Study or Reading

Grant me grace, O merciful God, to desire ardently all that is pleasing to Thee, to examine it prudently, to acknowledge it truthfully, and to accomplish it perfectly, for the praise and glory of Thy name. Amen.

Before Work

Look upon Thy servants, O Lord, and upon Thy works, and direct their children. And let the brightness of the Lord our God be upon us and direct Thou the works of our hands over us; yea, the work of our hands do Thou direct. Glory be to the Father, and to the Son, and to the Holy Ghost. As it was in the beginning, is now, and ever shall be, world without end. Amen.

For a Blessed Death

I beseech Thee, O Lord, to have mercy upon me at the last, and dispose the end of my life in peace; that it may be Christian, acceptable to Thee, fortified by Thy Sacraments, and, if it please Thee, painless. Gather me, O Lord, under the feet of Thine elect, when Thou wilt and as Thou wilt, only without sin and shame. Amen.

An Act of Faith

O my God, I firmly believe that Thou art one God in three Divine Persons, the Father, the Son, and the Holy Ghost; I believe that Thy Divine Son became man, and died for our sins, and that He will come to Judge the living and the dead. I believe these and all the truths which the Holy Orthodox Church teaches, because Thou hash revealed them, who canst neither deceive nor be deceived.

A Prayer for Faith, Hope and Charity

Almighty and everlasting God, give unto us the increase of faith, hope, and charity: and, that we may obtain that which Thou dost promise, make us to love that which Thou doest command. Through Jesus Christ our Lord. Amen.

Prayer Before a Crucifix

Look down upon me, good and gentle Jesus, while before Thy face I humbly kneel, and with burning soul pray and beseech Thee to fix deep in my heart lively sentiments of faith, hope and charity, true contrition for my sins, and a firm purpose of amend- ment. Meanwhile, I contemplate with great love and tender mercy Thy five most precious wounds, pondering over them within me, and calling to mind the words which David in prophecy made Thee say concerning Thyself, my Jesus: They have pierced My hands and feet; they have numbered all My bones.

- Our Lady of good studies, pray for us.
- Blessed be God!
- Thank God!
- God willing.
- My God and my all.
- Praised be Jesus Christ, now and forever more.
- My Jesus, Mercy!
- Lord, Jesus Christ, Son of God, have mercy on me a sinner.
- Jesus, Son of David, have mercy on me.
- He must increase and I must decrease.
- May thou father most just, most high, and most adorable will of God be done in all things, praised and magnified forever.

- Jesus in the Blessed Sacrament have mercy on us.
- Jesus, my God, I love Thee above all things.
- My Lord, grant that I may love Thee and that the reward of my love be to love Thee ever more and more.
- Eucharistic Heart of Jesus, increase in us our Faith, Hope and Charity.
- Saviour of the world, have mercy on us.
- My sweetest Jesus, be not my Judge, but my Saviour.
- Jesus, Mary, and Joseph, bless us now and at the hour of our death.
- "You did not choose me, but I chose you and appointed you that you should go and bear fruit and that your fruit should abide." *John 15:16*

PRAYERS BY A SICK PERSON

- Receive sickness as allowed by God, who allows such things to aid salvation.
- Look on sickness as a loving correction for sin, and as a summons to prepare for death.
- Have patience and submit to the will of God; repent and offer yourself to God to suffer greater pains if it will help you advance in holiness; give thanks for the blessings you enjoy.

25

- In dangerous illness, first send for a priest, make your confession, receive the sacraments, and ask for your name to be prayed at Mass.
- Ask for timely notice if the illness is dangerous and not flattered with false hope of recovery.
- Use your time wisely; admit but few visitors; settle temporal affairs.
- Dwell little on worldly matters, give yourself entirely to spiritual matters.
- Meditate often on our Lord's Passion.
- Bear in mind St. Augustine's words: "However innocent your life may have been, no Christian ought to, venture to die in any other state than that of a penitent."

Prayer in Suffering

O Lord Jesus Christ, accept my sufferings which I desire to unite with Thine. Sanctify this affliction so that every pang I feel may purify my soul and bring it nearer to Thee, to be made more one with Thee; grant that I may welcome the sufferings which will make me more like to Thee.

Prayer for Recovery

O Lord Jesus Christ, who didst go about doing good and healing all manner of disease amongst the people, lay Thy healing hand upon me, and if it be Thy will restore me to my former health. May Thy almighty strength support my weakness, and defend me from the enemy. May Thy sustaining presence be with me to sooth each ache and pain. O spare me a little, that I may recover my strength before I go hence and be no more seen. Heal me, O Lord, and I shall be healed. Save me, and I shall be saved, for Thou art my strength. Write, O Lord, Thy sacred wounds on my heart that I may never forget them, and that in them I may read Thy pains, that I may bear patiently every pain for Thee. Write Thy love on my heart that I may love only Thee. Lord, be merciful to me a sinner: Jesus, Son of the living God, have mercy upon me. I commend my soul to God my Creator, who made me out of nothing: to Jesus Christ my Saviour, who redeemed me with His precious Blood; to the Holy Ghost, who sanctified me in Baptism. Into Thy hands, O Lord, I commend my spirit. Let Thy holy angels defend me from all powers of darkness. Let Mary, Mother of God, and all the blessed Saints, pray for me a poor sinner.

Our Father...Hail Mary...

Glory be to the Father, and to the Son, and to the Holy Ghost. As it was in the beginning, is now, and ever shall be, world without end. Amen.

Christ, when Thou shalt call me hence, Be Thy Mother my defence, Be Thy Cross my victory.

For the Doctors and Nurses

O Lord and heavenly Father, I pray for the doctors and nurses, in whose care I lie. Give me the grace of faith, that I may ease their labours, and do Thou grant them good success. Especially do I pray for those of them who know Thee not, that they may be brought to the knowledge and love of Thee. Through Jesus Christ our Lord. Amen.

Before an Operation

O Lord Jesus Christ, who didst endure the scourging and wounding of Thy sacred body for our salvation, strengthen me to face this trial with serenity of mind, that I may bear witness to my sure trust in Thee. Bless the work of Thy servants, the doctors and nurses, that it may avail for the healing of my body and the purifying of my soul, through the merits of Thy sufferings. Amen.

Thanksgiving for Recovery

O Lord, God, give of life and health; I most heartily thank Thee, that in Thy mercy, Thou hast delivered me from sickness and affliction, and with a grateful heart I desire to offer unto Thy fatherly goodness myself, my Soul and body, to be a living sacrifice: unto Thee, always praising and magnifying Thy loving-kindness in the midst of Thy Church. Through Christ our Lord. Amen.

O Lord Jesus Christ, who came not to be ministered unto but to minister, I praise Thee for the blessings of medical science whereby my bodily health has been restored; give me grace to recognize that Thy ministry is continued by Priests, Pastors, and physicians, and that Thou art still the Good Physician of the souls and bodies of men. Who livest and reignest, world without end. Amen.

PRAYERS FOR THE SICK

For a Sick Person

Hear us, Almighty and most merciful God and Saviour; extend Thy accustomed goodness to this Thy servant who is grieved with sickness. Sanctify, we beseech Thee, this trial to him; that the sense of his weakness may add strength to his faith, and seriousness to his repentance. May it be Thy good pleasure to restore him to former health, that so he may live the rest of his life in Thy fear and to Thy glory.

For Healing

O God, who by the might of Thy command canst drive away from men's bodies all sickness and infirmity: be present in Thy goodness with this Thy servant, that his weakness being banished, and his health restored, he may live to glorify Thy Holy Name. Through Jesus Christ our Lord. Amen.

O Almighty God, who art the give of all health, and the aid of them that turn to Thee for succor: we entreat Thy strength and goodness in behalf of this Thy servant, that he may be healed of his infirmities, to Thine honour and glory, through Jesus Christ bur Lord. Amen.

O Christ our Lord, who art the Physician of Salvation, grant unto the sick the aid of heavenly healing. Look upon all faithful people who are sick, and take their souls into Thy keeping, and vouchsafe to deliver them from all infirmity; Who livest and reignest, world without end. Amen.

Prayer for the Suffering

O God, the Father of all look down in pity on those who suffer and heal the anguish of the world; release from the prison-house all held in the bondage of fear and set free such as are bound by the fetters of disease, whether of soul or body. Do Thou care for the desolate, give rest to the weary, comfort the sorrowful, watch by the sleepless, and to those who untended in their sickness grant the gentle ministry of angels, to supply their needs and relieve their pain. Visit with Thy great compassion all in their last agony and bring them in peace and safety into Thy Paradise of love. Through Jesus Christ our Lord. Amen.

For a Sick Child

O Lord Jesus Christ, who didst with joy receive and bless the children brought to Thee, give Thy blessing to this Thy child: In Thine own, time deliver him from his bodily pain, that he may live to serve Thee all his days. Who livest and reignest, world without end. Amen.

For a Convalescent

O Lord, whose compassions fail not, and whose mercies are new every morning: we give Thee hearty thanks that it hath pleased Thee to give to this our brother both relief from pain and hope of renewed health; continue, we beseech Thee, in him the good work that Thou hast begun; that, daily increasing in bodily strength, and humbly rejoicing in Thy goodness, he may so order his life and conversation as always to think and do such things as shall please Thee. Through Jesus Christ our Lord. Amen.

Before an Operation

O God, whose never-failing Providence ordereth things both in heaven and earth; hear the humble prayers of Thy servant and direct the hand of the surgeon and prosper his skill to a merciful and blessed issue. Through Jesus Christ our Lord. Amen.

Where There Appears Small Hope of Recovery

O Father of mercies, and God of all comfort, our only hope in time of need; we fly unto Thee for succour in behalf of this Thy servant lying in great weakness of body. Look graciously upon him, O Lord; and the more the outward man decayeth, strengthen him so much the more continually with Thy grace and Holy Ghost in the inner man. Give him unfeigned repentance for all the errors of his life past, and steadfast faith in Thy Son Jesus; that his sins may be done away by Thy mercy, and his pardon sealed in heaven; through the same Thy Son, our Lord and Saviour. Amen.

PRAISE AND THANKSGIVINGS

The Te Deum

We praise Thee, O God: we acknowledge Thee to be the Lord.

Thee, the Father everlasting, all the earth doth worship.

To Thee all angels; to Thee the heavens and all the powers:

To Thee the cherubim and seraphim continually cry: Holy, holy, holy, Lord God of Sabbaoth.

Heaven and earth are full of the majesty of Thy glory.

Thee, the glorious choir of the apostles,

Thee, the admirable company of the prophets,

Thee, the white-robed army of martyrs, praise.

Thee, the holy Church throughout the world doth acknowledge:

The Father of infinite majesty;

Thy adorable, true, and only Son;

Also, the Holy Ghost, the Comforter.

Thou, O Christ, art the King of glory,

Thou art the everlasting Son of the Father.

When Thou didst take upon Thee to deliver man,

Thou didst not disdain the Virgin's womb.

Having overcome the sting of death, Thou didst open the kingdom of Heaven to all believers.

Thou sittest at the right hand of God, in the glory of the Father.

We believe that Thou shalt come to be our Judge.

We therefore pray Thee to help Thy servants, whom Thou hast redeemed with Thy precious Blood.

Make them to be numbered with Thy saints in glory everlasting.

Save Thy people, O Lord, and bless Thy inheritance. Govern them, and raise them up forever.

Everyday we bless Thee.

And we praise Thy name forever; yea, forever and ever.

Vouchsafe, O Lord this day, to keep us from sin.

Have mercy on us, O Lord, have mercy on us.

℣. Blessed art Thou, O Lord, the God of our fathers.

℟. And worthy to be praised, and glorious forever.

℣. Let us bless the Father and the Son with the Holy Ghost.

℟. Let us praise and magnify Him forever.

℣. Blessed art Thou, O Lord, in the firmament of heaven.

℟. And worthy to be praised, glorified and exalted forever.

℣.Bless the Lord, O my soul.

℟. And forget not all His benefits.

℣.O Lord, hear my prayer.

℟. And let my cry come unto Thee.

℣.The Lord be with you.

℟. And with thy spirit.

Let us pray. O God, Whose mercies are without number, and the treasure of Whose goodness is infinite; we render thanks to Thy most gracious Majesty for the gifts Thou hast bestowed upon us, evermore beseeching Thy clemency; that as Thou grantest the petitions of those who ask Thee, Thou wilt never forsake them, but wilt prepare them for the rewards to come.

O God, Who hast taught the hearts of the faithful by the light of the Holy Ghost: grant us, by the same Ghost, to relish what is right, and evermore to rejoice in His consolation.

O God, Who sufferest none that hope in Thee to be afflicted overmuch, but dost listen graciously to their prayers; we render Thee thanks because Thou hast received our supplications and wishes, and we most humbly beseech Thee that we may evermore be protected from all adversities. Through Jesus Christ our Lord. Amen.

An Act of Praise

To God the Father, Who first loved us and made us accepted in the Beloved; to God the Son, Who loved us and washed us from our sins in His own Blood; to God the Holy Ghost, Who sheds the love of God abroad in our hearts-be all love, and all glory, for time and for eternity. Amen.

An Act of Thanksgiving

We thank Thee, O God, for blessings without number which we have received from Thee; chiefly for our creation, preservation, and all the blessings of this life; but above all for the Redemption of the world by our Lord Jesus Christ, for our regeneration by the Holy Ghost, and for our membership in the Orthodox Catholic Church. Through Christ our Lord. Amen.

A General Thanksgiving

Almighty God, Father of all mercies, we Thine unworthy servants do give Thee most humble and hearty thanks for all Thy goodness and loving-kindness to us, and to all men; We bless Thee for our creation, preservation, and all the blessings of this life; but above all for Thine inestimable love in the redemption of the world by our Lord Jesus Christ; for the means of grace and for the hope of glory. And, we beseech Thee, give us that due sense of all Thy mercies, that our hearts may be unfeignedly thankful, and that we show forth Thy praise, not only with our lips, but in our lives; by giving up ourselves to Thy service, and by walking before Thee in holiness and righteousness all our days. Through Jesus Christ our Lord. Amen.

Part 2

Spiritual Helps

Liturgical Year

- Advent (four Sundays before Christmas)
- Christmastide (Twelve Days of Christmas)
- Epiphanytide (week of Epiphany plus the variable weeks after Epiphany)
- Septuagesimatide (three Sundays before Lent)
- Lent (Ash Wednesday to Passion Sunday)
- Passiontide (Passion Week until Holy Thursday)
- Triduum (Holy Thursday, Friday, and Saturday)
- Eastertide (Easter to the end of Pentecost week)
- Per Annum, beginning on Trinity Sunday.

Abstinence

Abstinence includes forgoing meat and the juice thereof. It is customary for all who have attained the age of reason to abstain. Days of Abstinence include all Fridays, except when Christmas falls on a Friday.

Fasting

Fasting includes abstinence and adds to it the quantity of food. One may eat one full meal a day and not before noon. A collation (one-fourth of a meal) is also allowed. All who are +21 are to observe the fast.

- Mondays, Wednesdays and Fridays in Advent
- Every day in Lent, except Sundays
- Ember Days
- The vigils of Pentecost, Assumption, All Saints, and Christmas (if a Sunday, keep the day before).

The Seven Penitential Psalms
6,31,37,50,101,129,142

Psalm 6

O LORD, rebuke me not in thine indignation neither chasten me in thy displeasure.

2 Have mercy upon me, O Lord, for I am weak O Lord, heal me, for my bones are vexed.

3 My soul also is sore troubled but, Lord, how long wilt thou punish me?

4 Turn thee, O Lord, and deliver my soul O save me for thy mercy's sake.

5 For in death no man remembereth thee and who will give thee thanks in the pit?

6 I am weary of my groaning; every night wash I my bed and water my couch with my tears.

7 My beauty is gone for very trouble and worn away because of all mine enemies.

⁸ Away from me, all ye that work vanity for the Lord hath heard the voice of my weeping.

⁹ The Lord hath heard my petition the Lord will receive my prayer.

¹⁰ All mine enemies shall be confounded, and sore vexed they shall be turned back, and put to shame suddenly.

Psalm 31 (32)

REJOICE in the Lord, O ye righteous: for it becometh well the just to be thankful.

² Praise the Lord with harp: sing praises unto him with the lute, and instrument of ten strings.

³ Sing unto the Lord a new song: sing praises lustily unto him with a good courage.

⁴ For the word of the Lord is true: and all his works are faithful.

⁵ He loveth righteousness and judgement: the earth is full of the goodness of the Lord.

⁶ By the word of the Lord were the heavens made: and all the hosts of them by the breath of his mouth.

⁷ He gathereth the waters of the sea together, as it were upon an heap: and layeth up the deep, as in a treasure-house.

[8] Let all the earth fear the Lord: stand in awe of him, all ye that dwell in the world.

[9] For he spake, and it was done: he commanded and it stood fast.

[10] The Lord bringeth the counsel of the heathen to nought: and maketh the devices of the people to be of none effect, and casteth out the counsels of princes.

[11] The counsel of the Lord shall endure for ever: and the thoughts of his heart from generation to generation.

[12] Blessed are the people, whose God is the Lord Jehovah: and blessed are the folk, that he hath chosen to him to be his inheritance.

[13] The Lord looked down from heaven, and beheld all the children of men: from the habitation of his dwelling he considereth all them that dwell on the earth.

[14] He fashioneth all the hearts of them: and understandeth all their works.

[15] There is no king that can be saved by the multitude of an host: neither is any mighty man delivered by much strength.

[16] A horse is counted but a vain thing to save a man: neither shall he deliver any man by his great strength.

[17] Behold, the eye of the Lord is upon them that fear him: and upon them that put their trust in his mercy.

[18] To deliver their soul from death: and to feed them in the time of dearth.

[19] Our soul hath patiently tarried for the Lord: for he is our help and our shield.

[20] For our heart shall rejoice in him: because we have hoped in his holy Name.

[21] Let thy merciful kindness, O Lord, be upon us: like as we do put our trust in thee.

Psalm 37 (38)

I SAID, I will take heed to my ways, that I offend not in my tongue.

[2] I will keep my mouth as it were with a bridle, while the ungodly is in my sight.

[3] I held my tongue, and spake nothing I kept silence, yea, even from good words; but it was pain and grief to me.

[4] My heart was hot within me and while I was thus musing the fire kindled, and at the last I spake with my tongue:

[5] LORD, let me know mine end, and the number of my days; that I may be certified how long I have to live.

⁶ Behold, thou hast made my days as it were a span long, and mine age is even as nothing in respect of thee; and verily every man living is altogether vanity.

⁷ For man walketh in a vain shadow, and disquieteth himself in vain; he heapeth up riches, and cannot tell who shall gather them.

⁸ And now, Lord, what is my hope? truly my hope is even in thee.

⁹ Deliver me from all mine offences; and make me not a rebuke unto the foolish.

¹⁰ I became dumb, and opened not my mouth; for it was thy doing.

¹¹ Take thy plague away from me I am even consumed by the means of thy heavy hand.

¹²When thou with rebukes dost chasten man for sin, thou makest his beauty to consume away, like as it were a moth fretting a garment every man therefore is but vanity.

¹³ Hear my prayer, O LORD, and with thine ears consider my calling; hold not thy peace at my tears;

¹⁴For I am a stranger with thee, and a sojourner, as all my fathers were.

¹⁵O spare me a little, that I may recover my strength, before I go hence, and be no more seen.

Psalm 50 (51)

HAVE mercy upon me, O God, after thy great goodness according to the multitude of thy mercies do away mine offences.

2 Wash me throughly from my wickedness and cleanse me from my sin.

3 For I acknowledge my faults and my sin is ever before me.

4 Against thee only have I sinned, and done this evil in thy sight hat thou mightest be justified in thy saying, and clear when thou art judged.

5 Behold, I was shapen in wickedness and in sin hath my mother conceived me.

6 But lo, thou requirest truth in the inward parts and shalt make me to understand wisdom secretly.

7 Thou shalt purge me with hyssop, and I shall be clean thou shalt wash me, and I shall be whiter than snow.

8 Thou shalt make me hear of joy and gladness that the bones which thou hast broken may rejoice.

9 Turn thy face from my sins and put out all my misdeeds.

10 Make me a clean heart, O God and renew a right spirit within me.

[11] Cast me not away from thy presence and take not thy holy Spirit from me.

[12] O give me the comfort of thy help again and stablish me with thy free Spirit.

[13] Then shall I teach thy ways unto the wicked and sinners shall be converted unto thee.

[14] Deliver me from blood-guiltiness, O God, thou that art the God of my health and my tongue shall sing of thy righteousness.

[15] Thou shalt open my lips, O Lord and my mouth shall show thy praise.

[16] For thou desirest no sacrifice, else would I give it thee but thou delightest not in burnt-offerings.

[17] The sacrifice of God is a troubled spirit a broken and contrite heart, O God, shalt thou not despise.

[18] O be favourable and gracious unto Sion build thou the walls of Jerusalem.

[19] Then shalt thou be pleased with the sacrifice of righteousness, with the burnt-offerings and oblations then shall they offer young bullocks upon thine altar.

Psalm 101 (102)

HEAR my prayer, O Lord and let my crying come unto thee.

² Hide not thy face from me in the time of my trouble incline thine ear unto me when I call; O hear me, and that right soon.

³ For my days are consumed away like smoke and my bones are burnt up as it were a firebrand.

⁴ My heart is smitten down, and withered liked grass so that I forget to eat my bread.

⁵ For the voice of my groaning my bones will scarce cleave to my flesh.

⁶ I am become like a pelican in the wilderness and like an owl that is in the desert.

⁷ I have watched, and am even as it were a sparrow that sitteth alone upon the house-top.

⁸ Mine enemies revile me all the day long and they that are mad upon me are sworn together against me.

⁹ For I have eaten ashes as it were bread and mingled my drink with weeping.

¹⁰ And that because of thine indignation and wrath for thou hast taken me up, and cast me down.

¹¹ My days are gone like a shadow and I am withered like grass.

¹² But thou, O Lord, shalt endure for ever and thy remembrance throughout all generations.

¹³Thou shalt arise, and have mercy upon Sion for it is time that thou have mercy upon her, yea, the time is come.

¹⁴And why? thy servants think upon her stones and it pitieth them to see her in the dust.

¹⁵The heathen shall fear thy Name, O Lord and all the kings of the earth thy majesty;

¹⁶When the Lord shall build up Sion and when his glory shall appear;

¹⁷When he turneth him unto the prayer of the poor destitute and despiseth not their desire.

¹⁸This shall be written for those that come after and the people which shall be born shall praise the Lord.

¹⁹For he hath looked down from his sanctuary out of the heaven did the Lord behold the earth;

²⁰That he might hear the mournings of such as are in captivity and deliver the children appointed unto death;

²¹That they may declare the Name of the Lord in Sion and his worship at Jerusalem;

²²When the people are gathered together and the kingdoms also, to serve the Lord.

[23] He brought down my strength in my journey and shortened my days.

[24] But I said, O my God, take me not away in the midst of mine age as for thy years, they endure throughout all generations.

[25] Thou, Lord, in the beginning hast laid the foundation of the earth and the heavens are the work of thy hands.

[26] They shall perish, but thou shalt endure they all shall wax old as doth a garment;

[27] And as a vesture shalt thou change them, and they shall be changed but thou art the same, and thy years shall not fail.

[28] The children of thy servants shall continue and their seed shall stand fast in thy sight.

Psalm 129 (130)

OUT of the deep have I called unto thee, O Lord Lord, hear my voice.

[2] O let thine ears consider well the voice of my complaint.

[3] If thou, Lord, wilt be extreme to mark what is done amiss O Lord, who may abide it?

[4] For there is mercy with thee therefore shalt thou be feared.

⁵I look for the Lord; my soul doth wait for him in his word is my trust.

⁶My soul fleeth unto the Lord before the morning watch, I say, before the morning watch.

⁷O Israel, trust in the Lord, for with the Lord there is mercy and with him is plenteous redemption.

⁸And he shall redeem Israel from all his sins.

Psalm 142 (143)

HEAR my prayer, O Lord, and consider my desire hearken unto me for thy truth and righteousness' sake.

²And enter not into judgement with thy servant for in thy sight shall no man living be justified.

³For the enemy hath persecuted my soul; he hath smitten my life down to the ground he hath laid me in the darkness, as the men that have been long dead.

⁴Therefore is my spirit vexed within me and my heart within me is desolate.

⁵Yet do I remember the time past; I muse upon all thy works yea, I exercise myself in the works of thy hands.

⁶I stretch forth my hands unto thee my soul gaspeth unto thee as a thirsty land.

[7] Hear me, O Lord, and that soon, for my spirit waxeth faint hide not thy face from me, lest I be like unto them that go down into the pit.

[8] O let me hear thy loving-kindness betimes in the morning, for in thee is my trust show thou me the way that I should walk in, for I lift up my soul unto thee.

[9] Deliver me, O Lord, from mine enemies for I flee unto thee to hide me.

[10] Teach me to do a thing that pleaseth thee, for thou art my God let thy loving Spirit lead me forth into the land of righteousness.

[11] Quicken me, O Lord, for thy Name's sake and for thy righteousness' sake bring my soul out of trouble. [12] And of thy goodness slay mine enemies and destroy all them that vex my soul; for I am thy servant.

Part 3

The Mass

PRAYERS BEFORE MASS

In the Name of the Father and of the Son and of the Holy Ghost. Amen.

O great and good God, I have come into Thy presence to share in offering to Thee the great Sacrifice of Thy Blessed Son, our Saviour, Jesus Christ (and to receive the Holy Sacrament of the Body and Blood of the same Jesus Christ) in remembrance of His Life, Death, Passion, and Resurrection, and in thanksgiving for all Thy blessings bestowed upon Thy whole Church and on me a most unworthy sinner. I desire to receive with all the love and contrition of which I am capable, in conformity with those sacred intentions wherewith our Saviour instituted and our holy Mother Church ever offers it. I wish, then, to receive it:

For Thy greater glory. For the continual remembrance of the Sacrifice of Christ.

To give Thee thanks for all the blessings Thou hast bestowed, especially (names).

To ask Thy help in any matter I have in hand, especially (names).

To ask Thee to bless all my friends and relations, especially (names).

For the Dead, especially (names). Most gracious God, we beseech Thee mercifully to incline Thine ear unto our prayers: that our hearts being enlightened by the grace of thy Holy Ghost, we may duly serve Thee in these sacred mysteries, and be found worthy to cleave steadfastly unto Thy love.

Grant, O Lord, we pray thee, that the fire of Thy Holy Ghost may in such wise cleanse our reins and our hearts: that we, serving Thee in pureness both of body and soul, may be found an acceptable people in Thy sight.

We beseech Thee, O Lord, that the Comforter which proceedeth from Thee may enlighten our minds: and lead us, as Thy Son hath promised, into all truth.

Assist us mercifully, O Lord, with the might of Thy Holy Ghost: that by the gracious operation of the same, we may be purified inwardly from all our iniquities, and continually defended against all adversaries.

O God, who didst teach the hearts of Thy faithful people, by sending them the light of Thy Holy Ghost: grant us by the same Spirit to have a right judgement in all things, and evermore to rejoice in His holy comfort.

O Lord, we pray Thee that the visitation of Thy grace may in such wise cleanse our conscience from all sins: that Thy Son, our Lord Jesus Christ, when He cometh unto us, may find therein a mansion prepared for

Himself. Who liveth and reigneth with Thee in the unity of the Holy Ghost, ever one God, world without end. Amen.

For Priest and all the Faithful

Bless the priest through whom I am to make this oblation. Bless all the people who are here to participate in this glorious action and all who would like to be here. Convert all sinners. Heal the anguish of the world. And have mercy upon all the faithful departed. Accept all my prayers during this holy service of bur bounden duty, for Jesus Christ's sake. Amen.

For asking the Prayers of the Saints

Defend us, O Lord, we beseech Thee, from all dangers both of body and soul: and at the intercession of the blessed and glorious Ever-Virgin Mary, Mother of God, of blessed Joseph, of Thy holy Apostles Peter and Paul, of blessed N., and of all Thy Saints, grant us Thy saving health and peace; that being defended from all adversities and all false doctrines, Thy Church may serve Thee in freedom and quietness. Through Jesus Christ our Lord. Amen.

The Almighty and merciful Lord grant unto us joy with peace, amendment of life, time for true repentance, the grace and comfort of the Holy Ghost, and perseverance in good works. Amen.

PREPARATION FOR COMMUNION

When the Sunday or Feast is a double, the antiphon is said entirely; otherwise, the antiphon is said to the star (*).

Antiphon. Remember not, * Lord, our offenses, nor the offenses of our forefathers, neither take thou vengeance of our sins. (Eastertide: Alleluia)

Psalm 83. *Quam dilecta*
O how amiable are thy dwellings, thou Lord of hosts!

My soul hath a desire and longing to enter into the courts of the Lord; my heart and my flesh rejoice in the living God.

Yea, the sparrow hath found her an house, and the swallow a nest, where she may lay her young, even thy altars, O Lord of hosts, my King and my God.

Blessed are they that dwell in thy house; they will be always praising thee.

Blessed is the man whose strength is in thee, in whose heart are thy ways,

Who going through the vale of misery use it for a well; and the pools are filled with water.

They will go from strength to strength, and unto the God of gods appeareth every one of them in Sion.

O Lord God of hosts, hear my prayer; hearken, O God of Jacob.

Behold, O God our defender, and look upon the face of thine Anointed.

For one day in thy courts is better than a thousand.

I had rather be a doorkeeper in the house of my God, than to dwell in the tents of un-godliness.

For the Lord God is a light and defence; the Lord will give grace and worship, and no good thing shall he withhold from them that live a godly life.

O Lord God of hosts, blessed is the man that putteth his trust in thee.

Glory be to the Father and to the Son, and to the Holy Ghost.

As it was in the beginning, is now, and ever shall be, world without end. Amen.

Psalm 84. *Benedixisti, Domine*

Lord, thou art become gracious unto thy land; thou hast turned away the captivity of Jacob.

Thou hast forgiven the offence of thy people, and covered all their sins.

Thou hast taken away all thy displeasure, and turned thyself from thy wrathful indignation.

Turn us then, O God our Saviour, and let thine anger cease from us.

Wilt thou be displeased at us for ever? and wilt thou stretch out thy wrath from one generation to another?

Wilt thou not turn again, and quicken us, that thy people may rejoice in thee?

Show us thy mercy, O Lord, and grant us thy salvation.

I will hearken what the Lord God will say concerning me; for he shall speak peace unto his people, and to his saints, that they turn not again.

For his salvation is nigh them that fear him, that glory may dwell in our land.

Mercy and truth are met together; righteousness and peace have kissed each other.

Truth shall flourish out of the earth; and righteousness hath looked down from heaven.

Yea, the Lord shall show loving-kindness; and our land shall give her increase.

Righteousness shall go before him, and he shall direct his going in the way.

Glory be to the Father and to the Son, and to the Holy Ghost.

As it was in the beginning, is now, and ever shall be, world without end. Amen.

Psalm 85. *Inclina, Domine*

Bow down thine ear, O Lord, and hear me; for I am poor, and in misery.

Preserve thou my soul, for I am holy; my God, save thy servant that putteth his trust in thee.

Be merciful unto me, O Lord; for I will call daily upon thee.

Comfort the soul of thy servant; for unto thee, O Lord, do I lift up my soul.

For thou, Lord, art good and gracious, and of great mercy unto all them that call upon thee.

Give ear, Lord, unto my prayer, and ponder the voice of my humble desires.

In the time of my trouble I will call upon thee; for thou hearest me.

Among the gods there is none like unto thee, O Lord; there is not one that can do as thou doest.

All nations whom thou hast made shall come and worship thee, O Lord, and shall glorify thy Name.

For thou art great, and doest wondrous things; thou art God alone.

Teach me thy way, O Lord, and I will walk in thy truth; O knit my heart unto thee, that I may fear thy Name.

I will thank thee, O Lord my God, with all my heart, and will praise thy Name for evermore.

For great is thy mercy toward me; and thou hast delivered my soul from the nethermost hell.

O God, the proud are risen against me; and the congregations of naughty men have sought after my soul, and have not set thee before their eyes.

But thou, O Lord God, art full of compassion and mercy, long-suffering, plenteous in goodness and truth.

O turn thee then unto me, and have mercy upon me; give thy strength unto thy servant, and help the son of thine hand-maid.

Show some token upon me for good, that they who hate me may see it and be ashamed, because thou, Lord, hast holpen me and comforted me.

Glory be to the Father and to the Son, and to the Holy Ghost.

As it was in the beginning, is now, and ever shall be, world without end. Amen.

Psalm 115. *Credidi*

I believed, and therefore will I speak; but I was sore troubled. I said in my haste, All men are liars.

What reward shall I give unto the Lord for all the benefits that he hath done unto me?

I will receive the cup of salvation, and call upon the Name of the Lord.

I will pay my vows now in the presence of all his people: right dear in the sight of the Lord is the death of his saints.

Behold, O Lord, how that I am thy servant; I am thy servant, and the son of thine handmaid. Thou hast broken my bonds in sunder.

I will offer to thee the sacrifice of thanksgiving, and will call upon the Name of the Lord.

I will pay my vows unto the Lord, in the sight of all his people, in the courts of the Lord's house, even in the midst of thee, O Jerusalem. Praise the Lord.

Glory be to the Father and to the Son, and to the Holy Ghost.

As it was in the beginning, is now, and ever shall be, world without end. Amen.

Psalm 129. *De profundis*

Out of the deep have I called unto thee, O Lord; Lord, hear my voice.

O let thine ears consider well the voice of my complaint.

If thou, Lord, wilt be extreme to mark what is done amiss, O Lord, who may abide it?

For there is mercy with thee; therefore shalt thou be feared.

I look for the Lord; my soul doth wait for him. In his word is my trust.

My soul fleeth unto the Lord before the morning watch, I say, before the morning watch.

O Israel, trust in the Lord; for with the Lord there is mercy, and with him is plenteous redemption.

And he shall redeem Israel from all his sins.

Glory be to the Father and to the Son, and to the Holy Ghost.

As it was in the beginning, is now, and ever shall be, world without end. Amen.

Antiphon. Remember not, Lord, our offenses, nor the offenses of our forefathers, neither take thou vengeance of our sins. (Eastertide: Alleluia)

Kyrie, eléison. Christe, eléison. Kyrie, eléison.

Our Father. (silently until):

℣. And lead us not into temptation.

℟. But deliver us from evil.

℣. I said, Lord be merciful unto me.

℟. Heal my soul, for I have sinned against thee.

℣. Turn thee again, O Lord, at the last.

℟. And be gracious unto thy servants.

℣. O Lord, let thy mercy lighten upon us.

℟. As our trust is in thee.

℣. Let thy priests be clothed with righteous-ness.

℟. And let thy Saints sing with joyfulness.

℣. Cleanse thou me from my secret faults, O Lord.

℟. Keep thy servant also from presumptuous sins.

℣. O Lord, hear my prayer.

℟. And let my cry come unto thee.

℣. The Lord be with you.

℟. And with thy spirit.

Let us pray. Most gracious God, incline thy merciful ears unto our prayers, and enlighten our hearts by the grace of the Holy Spirit: that we may worthily serve at thy holy Mysteries, and love thee with an everlasting love.

Almighty God, unto whom all hearts are open, all desires known, and from whom no secrets are hid: cleanse the thoughts of our hearts by the inspiration of thy Holy Spirit, that we may perfectly love thee, and worthily magnify thy holy Name.

Enkindle, O Lord, our hearts and minds with the fire of the Holy Spirit: that we may serve thee with a chaste body, and please thee with a clean heart.

We beseech thee, O Lord, that the Comforter, who proceedeth from thee, may enlighten our minds: and lead us into all truth, as thy Son hath promised.

Let the power of the Holy Spirit come upon us, O Lord, we beseech thee: that he may both mercifully cleanse our hearts, and de-fend us from all adversities.

O God, who didst teach the hearts of thy faithful people, by sending to them the light of thy Holy Spirit: grant us by the same Spirit to have a right judgment in all things, and evermore to rejoice in His holy comfort.

Purify our consciences, we beseech thee, O Lord, by thy visitation: that our Lord Jesus Christ thy Son, when he cometh, may find in us a mansion prepared for himself. Who with thee, in the unity of the Holy Ghost, liveth and reigneth God, world without end. Amen.

A Prayer of Saint Ambrose the Bishop

Sunday

O Supreme High Priest and true Pontiff, Jesus Christ, who didst offer thyself to God the Father a pure and spotless Victim upon the Al-tar of the Cross for us miserable sinners, and who didst give us thy Flesh to eat and thy Blood to drink, and didst ordain that Mystery in the power of the Holy Spirit, saying, This do, as often as ye shall do it, in remembrance of me; I pray thee, by that same Blood of thine, the great price of our salvation; I pray thee, by that wonderful and unspeakable love wherewith thou didst vouchsafe to love us, miserable and unworthy, as to wash us from our sins in thy Blood; teach me, thy unworthy servant, whom among thy other gifts, not for my own merit, but only out of the worthiness of thy mercy, thou hast deigned to call to the priestly office; teach me, I pray thee, by thy Holy Spirit, to handle so great a Mystery with such reverence and honor, with such fear and devotion, as are due and fitting. Make me, through thy grace, always so to believe and understand, so to conceive and firmly hold, so to think and speak of this wondrous Mystery, as shall please thee and benefit my own soul. Let thy good Spirit enter into my heart, there silently to sound, and without clamor of words to speak all truth. For exceeding deep are thy Mysteries, and covered with a sacred veil. Of thy great mercy grant me to assist in the Solemnity of the Mass with a clean heart and a pure mind. Set free my heart from all unclean and unholy, all vain and hurtful thoughts. Defend me with the loving and faithful guard, the mighty protection of thy blessed Angels, that the enemies of all good may go away ashamed. By the virtue of this great Mystery, and by the hand of thy holy Angel, drive away from me and from all thy servants the hard spirit of pride and vainglory, of impurity and uncleanness, of doubting and mistrust. Let them be confounded that persecute us: let them perish that make haste to destroy us.

Another Prayer of Saint Ambrose

To the Table of thy most sweet Feast, O loving Lord Jesus Christ, I, a sinner, presuming nothing on my own merits, but trusting in thy mercy and goodness, approach with fear and trembling. For my heart and my body are stained with many and grievous sins, my thoughts and my lips have not been carefully kept. Wherefore, O gracious God, O awful Majesty, I, in my misery, being brought into a great strait, turn to thee, the Fountain of mercy, to thee I hasten to be healed, and flee under thy protection: and thee, before whom I cannot stand as my Judge, I long to have as my Savior. To thee, O Lord, I show my wounds, to thee I discover my shame. I know my sins, many and great, for which I am afraid: but I hope in thy mercies, of which there is no end. Look therefore upon me with the eyes of thy mercy, O Lord Jesus Christ, eternal King, God and Man, crucified for man. Hearken unto me whose trust is in thee: have mercy upon me who am full of misery and sin, thou Fountain of mercy that will never cease to flow. Hail, Victim of Salvation, offered for me and for all mankind upon the Altar of the Cross! Hail, noble and precious Blood, flowing from the wounds of my crucified Lord Jesus Christ, and washing away the sins of the whole world! Remember, O Lord, thy creature, whom thou hast redeemed with thine own Blood. It repents me that I have sinned, and I desire to amend what I have done. Take away therefore from me, O most merciful Father, all my sins and iniquities; that being purified both in soul and body, I may be made meet worthily to taste the Holy of Holies; and grant that this holy foretaste of thy Body and Blood, which I, unworthy, purpose to take, may be for the remission of my sins; the perfect cleansing of my faults; the driving away of shameful thoughts, and the renewal of good desires; the healthful performance of works well-pleasing unto thee; and the most sure protection of soul and body against the wiles of my enemies. Amen.

Almighty, everlasting God, lo, I draw nigh to the Sacrament of thine only begotten Son, our Lord Jesus Christ. I draw nigh as one sick, to the Physician of life; unclean, to the Fountain of mercy; blind, to the light of eternal brightness; poor and needy, to the Lord of heaven and earth. I implore, therefore, the abundance of thine exceeding bounty, that thou wouldest vouchsafe to heal my sickness, to wash my defilements, to enlighten my blindness, to enrich my poverty, and to clothe my nakedness; and that I may receive the Bread of Angels, the King of kings, the Lord of lords, with such reverence and humility, such contrition and devotion, such purity and faith, and with such purpose and intention, as shall be expedient for the health of my soul. Grant me, I beseech thee, that I may receive not only the Sacrament of the Body and Blood of the Lord, but also the substance and virtue of the Sacrament. O most merciful God, grant me so to receive the body of thine only begotten Son our Lord Jesus Christ, which he took of the Virgin Mary, that I may be worthy to be incorporated into his mystical Body and accounted among his members. O most loving Father, grant me, that thy beloved Son, whom I now purpose to receive veiled from sight, I may at length behold forever face to face. Who with thee, in the unity of the Holy Ghost, liveth and reigneth God, world without end. Amen.

Prayer to the Blessed Virgin Mary

O Most Blessed Virgin Mary, mother of gentleness and mercy, I, a miserable and unworthy sinner, flee to thy protection with every sentiment of humility and love; and I implore of thy loving kindness that thou wouldst vouchsafe graciously to be near me, and all who throughout the whole Church are to receive the Body and Blood of thy Son this day, even as thou wert near thy sweetest Son as He hung bleeding on the Cross, that, aided by thy gracious help, we may worthily offer up a pure and acceptable sacrifice in the sight of the Holy and Undivided Trinity. Amen.

Prayer to Saint Joseph

Happy and blessed art thou, O Joseph, to whom it was given not only to see and to hear that God whom many kings desired to see, and saw not, to hear, and heard not; but also to bear him in thine arms, to embrace him, to clothe him, and to guard and defend him.

℣. Pray for us, O Blessed Joseph.
℟. That we may be made worthy of the promises of Christ.

Let us pray. O GOD, who hast given unto us a royal Priesthood, vouchsafe, we beseech thee that as blessed Joseph was found worthy to hold with his hands and bear within in his arms, thine only begotten Son, born of the Virgin Mary, so may we be made fit, by cleanness of heart and innocency of works, to wait upon thy Holy Altars; that we may worthily receive the Most Sacred Body and Blood of thy Son, now in this present life, and deserve to attain an everlasting reward in the world to come. Through the same Christ, our Lord.

Prayer to all the Angels and Saints

ANGELS, Archangels, Thrones, Dominations, Principalities, Powers and Virtues of the heavens, Cherubim and Seraphim, and all ye Saints of God, especially my Patrons, vouchsafe to intercede for me, that I may be enabled worthily to receive this sacrifice to almighty God, to the praise and glory of His holy Name, for my benefit, and that of all his holy Church. Amen.

Prayer to Saint(s) in whose honor the Mass is celebrated.

O Holy N(s)., behold I, a miserable sinner, trusting in your merits, intend to receive the most holy Sacrament of the Body and Blood of our Lord Jesus Christ for your honor and glory. I humbly and devoutly pray: vouchsafe this day to intercede for me, that I may be enabled worthily and acceptably to receive so great a sacrifice; that with thee and all His elect I may praise him eternally and reign with him: Who liveth and reigneth, world without end. Amen.

Declaration of Intention Before Mass

I intend to assist at this celebration of the Mass, and at the consecration the Body and Blood of our Lord Jesus Christ, according to the rite of the holy Church of Rome, to the praise of Almighty God, and the whole Church triumphant; for my own benefit; for the benefit of the whole Church militant and expectant; for all who have commended themselves to my prayers in general and in particular Nn.; and for the good estate of the holy Church.

The almighty and merciful Lord grant unto us joy with peace, amendment of life, time for true repentance, the grace and comfort of the Holy Ghost, and perseverance in good works. Amen.

LITURGY KEY

✠ = sign of the cross
A = a response from the altar servers
P = reserved for the priest
℟. = a response from the congregation
ALL CAPS = genuflect, if standing

THE SPRINKLING OF HOLY WATER

THE ASPERGES (throughout the year, Glory be is omitted in Passion tide)
P. Thou shalt purge me.

℟. O Lord, with hyssop, and I shall be clean: thou shalt wash me, and I shall be whiter than snow. Have mercy upon me, O God: after thy great goodness. Glory be to the Father, and to the Son and to the Holy Ghost: as it was in the beginning, is now and ever shall be, world without end. Amen

VIDI AQUAM (in Paschaltide)

P. I beheld water.

℟. Which proceeded from the temple, on the right side thereof, alleluia: and all they to whom that water came were healed everyone one, and they say, alleluia, alleluia. O give thanks unto the Lord, for he is gracious: and his mercy endureth forever. Glory be to the Father, and to the Son and to the Holy Ghost: as it was in the beginning, is now and ever shall be, world without end. Amen

Then continue...

P. O Lord, show thy mercy upon us (alleluia).
℟. And grant us thy salvation (alleluia).
P. O Lord, hear my prayer.
℟. And let my cry come unto Thee.
P. The Lord be with you.
℟. And with thy spirit.
P. Let us pray. Graciously hear us, O Lord, holy Father, almighty everlasting God: and vouchsafe to send thy Holy Angel from heaven; to guard and cherish, protect and visit, and to defend all who dwell in this thy holy habitation. Through Christ our Lord.
℟. Amen.

THE LITURGY OF ST. TIKHON

ORDINARY OF THE LITURGY:

THE INTROIT

COLLECTS OF PURITY
AND THE SUMMARY OF THE LAW

P. Almighty God, unto whom all hearts are open, all desires known, and from whom no secrets are hid; cleanse the thoughts of our hearts by the inspiration of thy Holy Ghost, that we may perfectly love thee, and worthily magnify thy Holy Name; through Christ our Lord.

℟. Amen.

P. Hear what our Lord Jesus Christ saith. Thou shalt love the Lord thy God with all thy heart, and with all thy soul, and with all thy mind. This is the first and great commandment. And the second is like unto it;

Thou shalt love thy neighbor as thyself. On these two commandments hang all the Law and the Prophets.

THE KYRIE

Lord, have mercy upon us. (Kyrie, eleison)
Lord, have mercy upon us. (Kyrie, eleison)
Lord, have mercy upon us. (Kyrie, eleison)
Christ, have mercy upon us. (Christe, eleison)
Christ, have mercy upon us. (Christe, eleison)
Christ, have mercy upon us. (Christe, eleison)
Lord, have mercy upon us. (Kyrie, eleison)
Lord, have mercy upon us. (Kyrie, eleison)
Lord, have mercy upon us. (Kyrie, eleison)

THE GLORIA

The Gloria is omitted during Advent and Lent

P. Glory be to God on high.

℟. And on earth peace, towards men of good will. We praise thee. We bless thee. We worship thee. We glorify thee. We give thanks to thee for thy great glory. O Lord God, heavenly king, God the Father almighty. O Lord, the only begotten Son, Jesus Christ. O Lord God, Lamb of God, Son of the Father. That takest away the sins of the world, have mercy upon us. Thou that takest away the sins of the world, receive our prayer. Thou that sittest at the right hand of the Father, have mercy upon us. For thou only art holy. Thou only art the Lord. Thou only, O Jesus Christ, with the Holy Ghost, ✠ art most high in the glory of God the Father. Amen.

P. The Lord be with you.

℟. And with thy spirit.

P. Let us pray. *The Collects*

THE EPISTLE

A. The Reading is from (name).

℟. Thanks be to God.

THE GRADUAL AND ALLELUIA

During Paschal Tide, the Gradual is replaced with a second Alleluia. During Lent, the Alleluia is re-placed with the Tract.

THE GOSPEL

P. The Lord be with you.

℟. And with thy spirit.

P. The beginning (or The continuation) of the holy Gospel according to N.

℟. Glory be to Thee, O Lord.

P. (the priest/deacon reads the gospel)

℟. Praise be to Thee, O Christ.

THE NICENE CREED

P. I BELIEVE IN ONE GOD

℟. The Father almighty, Maker of heaven and earth, and of all things visible and invisible. And in one Lord Jesus Christ, the only begotten Son of God. Begotten of the Father before all worlds. God of God, Light of Light, very God of very God. Begotten, not made, being of one substance with the Father: by whom all things were made. Who for us men and for our salvation, came down from heaven, AND WAS INCARNATE BY THE HOLY GHOST OF THE VIRGIN MARY: AND WAS MADE MAN, and was crucified also for us: under Pontius Pilate he suffered and was buried. And the third day he rose again according to the Scriptures. And ascended into heaven: and sitteth on the right hand of the Father. And he shall come again with glory, to judge both the quick and the dead: whose kingdom shall have no end.

And I believe in the Holy Ghost, the Lord and Giver of life: who proceedeth from the Father. Who with the Father and the Son together is worshipped and glorified: who spake by the prophets. And I believe in one holy Catholic and Apostolic Church. I acknowledge one Baptism for the remission of sins. And I look for the resurrection of the dead, and the life ✠ of the world to come. Amen.

THE OFFERTORY

P. The Lord be with you.

℟. And with thy spirit.

P. Let us pray. (offertory verse and hymns)

P. Pray, brethren, that my sacrifice and yours may be acceptable to God the Father almighty.

℟. May the Lord receive the sacrifice at thy hands, to the praise and glory of His Name, to our benefit also, and that of all his holy Church.

MEMORIALS

P. Let us pray for the whole state of Christ's Church.

Almighty and ever living God, who by thy holy Apostle hast taught us to make prayers, and supplications, and to give thanks for all men: We humbly beseech thee most mercifully to accept (these) our Oblations, and to receive these our prayers, which we offer unto thy Divine Majesty: beseeching thee to inspire continually the Universal Church with the spirit of truth, unity, and concord: And grant that all those who do confess thy holy name may agree in the truth of thy holy Word, and live in unity and godly love. We beseech thee also, so to direct and dispose the hearts of all Christian Rulers, that they may truly and impartially administer justice, to the punishment of wickedness and vice, and to the maintenance of thy true religion and virtue. Give grace, O heavenly Father, to all Bishops and other Ministers, especially our Father and Metropolitan (name), that they may, both by their life and doctrine, set forth thy true and lively Word, and rightly and duly administer thy holy Sacraments. And to all thy people give thy heavenly grace; and especially to this congregation here present; that, with meek heart and due reverence, they may hear, and receive thy holy Word; truly serving thee in holiness and righteousness all the days of their life. And we most humbly beseech thee, of thy goodness, O Lord, to comfort and succor all those who, in this transitory life, are in trouble, sorrow, need, sickness, or any other adversity (names). And we also bless thy holy name for all thy servants departed this life in thy faith and fear; beseeching thee to grant them continual growth in thy love and service. And give us grace so to follow the good examples of blessed Mary and all thy Saints, that, through their intercessions, we (with them) may be partakers of thy heavenly kingdom. Grant this, O Father, for Jesus Christ's sake, our only Mediator and Advocate. Amen.

COMMUNION DEVOTIONS

P. Ye who do truly and earnestly repent you of your sins, and are in love and charity with your neighbors, and intend to lead a new life, following the commandments of God, and walking from henceforth in his holy ways; Draw near with faith, and take this holy Sacrament to your comfort; and make your humble confession to Almighty God, devoutly kneeling.

℟. ALMIGHTY God, Father of our Lord Jesus Christ, maker of all things, judge of all men; We acknowledge and bewail our manifold sins and wickedness, which we from time to time most grievously have committed, By thought, word, and deed, against thy Divine Majesty, Provoking most justly thy wrath and indignation against us. We do earnestly repent, and are heartily sorry for these our misdoings; The remembrance of them is grievous unto us; the burden of them is intolerable. Have mercy upon us, have mercy upon us, most merciful Father; For thy Son our Lord Jesus Christ's sake, forgive us all that is past and grant that we may ever hereafter serve and please thee in newness of life.

To the honor and glory of thy Name; through Jesus Christ our Lord. Amen.

P. Almighty God, our heavenly Father, who of His great mercy hath promised forgiveness of sins to all those who with hearty repentance and true faith turn unto him; have mercy upon you; pardon and deliver you from all your sins; confirm and strengthen you in all goodness; and bring you to everlasting life; through Jesus Christ our Lord. Amen.

Hear what comfortable words our Saviour Christ saith unto all who truly turn to him.

Come unto me, all ye that travail and are heavy laden, and I will refresh you.

So God loved the world, that he gave His only-begotten Son, to the end that all that believe in him should not perish, but have everlasting life.

Hear also what St. Paul saith. This is a true saying, and worthy of all men to be received, that Christ Jesus came into the world to save sinners.

Hear also what St. John saith. If any man sin, we have an advocate with the Father, Jesus Christ the righteous; and he is the propitiation for our sins.

SURSUM CORDA

P. The Lord be with you.

℟. And with thy spirit.

P. Lift up your hearts.

℟. We lift them up unto the Lord.

P. Let us give thanks unto our Lord God.

℟. It is meet and right so to do.

PREFACE of the Trinity

P. It is very meet, right, and our bounden duty, that we should at all times, and in all places, give thanks unto thee, O Lord, holy Father, almighty, everlasting God: Who with thine only-begotten Son and the Holy Ghost art one God, one Lord: not one only Person, but three Persons in one Substance. For that which we believe of thy glory, O Father, the same we believe of thy Son, and of the Holy Ghost, without any difference or inequality. Therefore with Angels and Archangels, and with all the company of heaven, we laud and magnify thy glorious name: evermore praising thee, and saying:

THE SANCTUS

Holy, Holy, Holy Lord God of hosts: Heaven and earth are full of thy glory. Glory be to thee, O Lord Most High. ✠ Blessed is he that cometh in the Name of the Lord. Hosanna in the highest.

CANON OF THE EUCHARIST

Consecration

P. All glory be to thee, Almighty God, our heavenly Father, for that thou, of thy tender mercy, didst give thine only Son Jesus Christ to suffer death upon the Cross for our redemption; who (by his own oblation of himself once offered) made a full, perfect, and sufficient sacrifice, oblation, and satisfaction, for the sins of the whole world; and did institute, and in his holy Gospel command us to continue, a perpetual memory of that his precious death and sacrifice, until his coming again:

For in the night in which he was betrayed, he took bread; and when he had given thanks, he brake it, and gave it to his disciples, saying,

TAKE, EAT, THIS IS MY BODY,
WHICH IS GIVEN FOR YOU;
DO THIS IN REMEMBRANCE OF ME.

Likewise, after supper, he took the cup; and when he had given thanks, he gave it to them, saying,

DRINK YE ALL OF THIS;
FOR THIS IS MY BLOOD
OF THE NEW TESTAMENT,
WHICH IS SHED FOR YOU, AND FOR MANY,
FOR THE REMISSION OF SINS;
DO THIS AS OFT AS YE SHALL DRINK IT,
IN REMEMBRANCE OF ME.

Oblation

Wherefore, O Lord and heavenly Father, according to the institution of thy dearly beloved Son, our Saviour, Jesus Christ, we, thy humble servants, do celebrate and make here before thy Divine Majesty, with these thy holy gifts, which we now offer unto thee, the memorial thy Son hath commanded us to make; having in remembrance his blessed passion and precious death, his mighty resurrection and glorious ascension;

rendering unto thee most hearty thanks for the innumerable benefits procured unto us by the same.

Epiclesis

And we most humbly beseech thee, O merciful Father, to hear us; and of thy almighty goodness, vouchsafe to send down thy Holy Ghost upon these thy gifts and creatures of bread and wine, that they may be changed into the Body and Blood of thy most dearly beloved Son. Grant that we, receiving them according to thy Son our Saviour Jesus Christ's holy institution, in remembrance of his death and passion, may be partakers of his most blessed Body and Blood. And we earnestly desire thy fatherly goodness, mercifully to accept this our sacrifice of praise and thanksgiving; most humbly beseeching thee to grant that, by the merits and death of thy Son Jesus Christ, and through faith in his blood, we, and all thy whole Church, may obtain remission of our sins, and all other benefits of his passion. And here we offer and present unto thee, O Lord, ourselves, our souls and bodies, to be a reasonable, holy, and living sacrifice unto thee; humbly beseeching thee, that we, and all others who shall be partakers of this holy Communion, may worthily receive the most precious Body and Blood of thy Son Jesus Christ, be filled with thy grace and heavenly benediction, and made one body with him, that he may dwell in us, and we in him. Be mindful also, O Lord, of thy servants who are gone before us with the sign of faith, and who rest in the sleep of peace, especially (names of the departed). To them, O Lord, and to all who rest in Christ grant we pray thee a place of refreshment, light and peace. To us sinners also, thy servants, confiding in the multitude of thy mercies, grant some lot and partnership with thy holy Apostles and martyrs (John, Stephen, Matthias, Barnabas, Ignatius, Alexander, Marcellinus, Peter, Felicitas, Perpetua, Agatha, Lucia, Agnes, Cecilia, Anastasia, and with all thy Saints) into whose company we pray thee of thy mercy to admit us. And although we are unworthy, through our manifold sins, to offer unto thee any sacrifice; yet we beseech thee to accept this our bounden duty and service; not weighing our merits, but pardoning our offenses, through Jesus Christ our Lord; by whom, and with whom, in the unity of the Holy Ghost, all honor and glory be unto thee, O Father Almighty, world without end. Amen.

THE LORD'S PRAYER

P. Let us pray. And now, as our Saviour Christ hath taught us, we are bold to say,

℟. Our Father who art in heaven, hallowed be thy name, thy kingdom come, thy will be done, on earth as it is in heaven. Give us this day our daily bread. And forgive us our trespasses, as we forgive those who trespass against us. And lead us not into temptation, but deliver us from evil. For thine is the kingdom, and the power, and the glory, for ever and ever. Amen.

P. Deliver us, we beseech thee, O Lord, from all evils, past, present, and to come: and at the intercession of the blessed and glorious ever-Virgin Mary, Mother of God, with thy blessed Apostles Peter and Paul, and with Andrew and all thy Saints, graciously give peace in our days that aided by the help of thy loving-kindness, we may ever both be free from sin and safe from all disquietude. Through the same thy Son our Lord Jesus Christ, who liveth and reigneth with thee in the unity of the Holy Spirit, ever one God, world without end.

℟. Amen.

P. The peace of the Lord be always with you.

℟. And with thy spirit.

THE AGNUS DEI

O Lamb of God, that takest away the sins of the world: Have mercy upon us. (repeat once)

O Lamb of God, that takest away the sins of the world: Grant us thy peace.

THE PAX

P. Peace be with thee.

℞. And with thy spirit.

PRAYER OF HUMBLE ACCESS

℞. We do not presume to come to this thy Table, O merciful Lord, trusting in our own righteousness, but in thy manifold and great mercies. we are not worthy so much as to gather up the crumbs under thy Table. But thou art the same Lord, whose property is always to have mercy: grant us therefore, gracious Lord, so to eat the flesh of thy dear Son Jesus Christ, and to drink his blood, that our sinful bodies may be made clean by his body, and our souls washed through his most precious blood, and that we may evermore dwell in him, and he in us. Amen.

P. Behold, the Lamb of God. Behold him that takest away the sins of the world.

P. Lord, I am not worthy, that thou shouldest come under my roof:

℟. but speak the word only, and my soul shall be healed. (three times)

THE COMMUNION PRAYER

℟. I believe, O Lord, and I confess that Thou art truly the Christ, the Son of the Living God, Who didst come into the world to save sinners, of whom I am chief. And I believe that this is truly Thine own immaculate Body, and that this is truly Thine own precious Blood. Therefore I pray Thee: have mercy upon me and forgive my transgressions both voluntary and involuntary, of word and of deed, of knowledge and of ignorance. And make me worthy to partake without condemnation of Thy immaculate Mysteries, for the remission of my sins, and unto life everlasting. Amen.

Of Thy Mystical Supper, O Son of God, accept me today as a communicant; for I will not speak of Thy Mystery to Thine enemies, neither like Judas will I give Thee a kiss; but like the thief will I confess Thee: Remember me, O Lord in Thy Kingdom, not unto judgment, nor unto condemnation, be my partaking of thy holy mysteries O Lord, but unto the healing of soul and body. Amen.

PRAYER OF THANKSGIVING

P. Let us pray.

℟. ALMIGHTY and ever living God, we most heartily thank thee, for that thou dost vouchsafe to feed us who have duly received these holy mysteries, with the spiritual food of the most precious Body and Blood of thy Son our Saviour Jesus Christ; and dost assure us thereby of thy favor and goodness towards us; and that we are very members incorporate in the mystical body of thy Son, which is the blessed company of all faithful people; and are also heirs through hope of thy everlasting kingdom, by the merits of his most precious death and passion. And we humbly beseech thee, O heavenly Father, so to assist us with thy grace, that we may continue in that holy fellowship, and do all such good works as thou hast prepared for us to walk in; through Jesus Christ our Lord, to whom, with thee and the Holy Ghost, be all honor and glory, world without end. Amen.

P. The Lord be with you.

℟. And with thy spirit.

P. Let us pray. *(Post-Communion prayers)*

DISMISSAL

P. The Lord be with you.

℟. And with thy spirit.

P. The Mass has ended. Depart in peace. *(if the Gloria was said)*

OR

P. Let us bless the Lord. (if the Gloria was not said)

℟. Thanks be to God.

THE BLESSING

P. (kneel) The Peace of God, which passeth all understanding, keep your hearts and minds in the knowledge and love of God, and of his Son, Jesus Christ our Lord: and the Blessing of God Almighty, the Father, the Son, and the Holy Ghost.

℟. Amen. (stand)

P. The Lord be with you.

℟. And with thy spirit.

P. The Beginning of the Holy Gospel according to John.

℟. Glory be to Thee, O Lord.

P. In the beginning was the Word, and the Word was with God, and the Word was God. The same was in the beginning with God. All things were made by Him; and without Him was not anything made that was made; in Him was life, and the life was the light of men; and the light shineth in darkness, and the darkness comprehended it not. There was a man sent from God, whose name was John. The same came for a witness, to bear witness of the light, that all men through him might believe. He was not that light but was sent to bear witness of that light. That was the true light, which lighteth every man that cometh into the world. He was in the world, and the world was made by Him, and the world knew Him not. He came unto His own, and His own received Him not. But as many as received Him, to them gave He power to become the sons of God, even to them that believe on His Name; which were born, not of blood, nor of the will of the flesh, nor of the will of man, but of God. AND THE WORD WAS MADE FLESH and dwelt among us; and we beheld His glory, the glory as of the Only-begotten of the Father, full of grace and truth.

℟. Thanks be to God.

THANKSGIVING AFTER COMMUNION

Blessed, praised, worshipped and adored be our Lord
Jesus Christ on His Throne of Glory in heaven, and in
the Most Holy Sacrament of the Altar.

May the souls of the faithful departed, through the
mercy of God, rest in peace. Amen.

Thanksgiving to the Holy Trinity

We thank Thee, almighty Father, who has prepared
holy Church to be a haven of rest for us and a temple
of holiness where Thou, in Thy most glorious Holy
Trinity, art glorified. (In Paschaltide add: Alleluia.)

We thank Thee, Christ our King, who hast bestowed
upon us life by Thy life-giving Body and holy Blood.
Grant us forgiveness and Thy great mercy. (In
Paschaltide add: Alleluia.)

We thank Thee, Spirit of Truth, who hast renewed
holy Church. Keep her faith in Thee, the most
glorious Holy Trinity, unblemished henceforth
through all ages, world without end. (In Paschaltide
add: Alleluia.) Amen.

Prayer to the Blessed Virgin Mary

O Mary, Virgin and Mother most holy, who wast
worthy to bear in thy womb the Creator of all things,
and to feed at thy breast Him whose true, real and

most holy Body and Blood I have now received: Vouchsafe, I beseech thee, to intercede for me, that I may henceforth render Him faithful service and persevere to the end in loving companionship with Him, so that, at the last, I may, with thee, praise and adore Him through all ages, world without end. Amen.

Prayer to the Saint(s) in Whose Honour Mass Has Been Celebrated

Holy N., to whose honour I have this day offered the bloodless sacrifice of the Body and Blood of Christ: Grant that, by thy powerful intercession before God, I may through the use of this mystery obtain the merits of the Passion, Death and Resurrection of the same Christ our Saviour, and that continually coming thereunto, I may ever set forward the work of my salvation. Amen.

An Oblation of Self

Accept, O Lord, my entire liberty, my memory, my understanding, and my will. All that I am and have thou hast given me; and I give all back to Thee to be disposed of according to Thy good pleasure. Give me only the comfort of Thy presence and the joy of Thy love; with these I shall be more than rich and shall desire nothing more.

Part 4

Devotions

THE ROSARY OF THE BLESSED VIRGIN MARY

Meditate on the 3rd Mystery, say "Our Father," "Hail Mary" 10x, and the "Glory be"

Meditate on the 4th Mystery, say "Our Father," "Hail Mary" 10x, and the "Glory be"

Meditate on the 2nd Mystery, say "Our Father," "Hail Mary" 10x, and the "Glory be"

Meditate on the 5th Mystery, say "Our Father," "Hail Mary" 10x, and the "Glory be"

Meditate on the 1st Mystery, say "Our Father," "Hail Mary" 10x, and the "Glory be"

Concluding Prayers: Antiphon of the B.V.M. according to season with its Collect

Say "Hail Mary" 3x and the "Glory be"

Say "Our Father"

Make the sign of the Cross, say the Apostles' Creed.

Manner of Saying the Rosary

1. Hold the cross in the right hand and bless yourself with the cross, saying, "In the Name of the Father, and of the Son, and of the Holy Ghost. Amen."

2. Still holding the cross, say the *Apostles' Creed.*

3. On the first large bead after the cross, say the *Our Father;* on the next three small beads, say the *Hail Mary;* after the third *Hail Mary,* say the *Glory be* on the chain.

4. Then name the mystery upon which you are to meditate; e.g., "The Annunciation."

5. While meditating on this mystery say the *Our Father* on the large bead just before the medal and the *Hail Mary* on the next ten small beads after the medal; adding after the tenth *Hail Mary* the *Glory be* on the chain.

6. Then proceed to the second mystery, saying the *Our Father* on the large bead and ten *Hail Marys* on the small beads, ending with *Glory be.* Continue until the set of mysteries has been finished.

7. Then say for concluding prayers the proper Antiphon of the Blessed Virgin according to the season.

Make the Sign of the Cross, say the Apostles' Creed. Say three "Hail Marys" and the Glory Be". Meditate on 1st Mystery, say "Our Father," ten "Hail Marys," and the "Glory Be". Repeat for each Mystery.

Concluding Prayers: Antiphon of the B.V.M. according to season with its Collect.

The Joyful Mysteries
Said on Mondays, Thursdays, and Sundays in Advent

I. The Annunciation, *St. Luke 1:26-38*
Let us contemplate, in this Mystery, how the Archangel Gabriel saluted our Blessed Lady with the title, Full of grace, and declared unto her the Incarnation of our Lord, God, and Saviour Jesus Christ.

Our Father. Hail Mary (10 times). Glory be.

Let us pray. O holy Mary, Queen of Virgins, through the most high Mystery of the Incarnation of thy beloved Son, our Lord Jesus Christ, wherein our salvation was begun; obtain for us, through thy most holy intercession, light to understand the greatness of the benefit He hath bestowed upon us, in vouchsafing to become our Brother, and in giving thee, His own beloved Mother, to be our Mother also. Amen.

II. The Visitation, *St. Luke 1:39-56*
Let us contemplate, in this Mystery, how the Blessed Virgin Mary, understanding from the Angel that her cousin St. Elizabeth had conceived, went with haste

95

into the mountains of Judea to visit her, and remained with her three months.

Our Father. Hail Mary (10 times). Glory be.

Let us pray. O holy Virgin, spotless Mirror of humility, by that exceeding love which moved thee to visit thy holy cousin St. Elizabeth, obtain for us, through thine intercession, that our hearts being visited by thy divine Son, and freed from all sin we may praise and thank Him for ever. Amen.

III. Nativity, *St. Luke 2:4-20; St. Matt. 2:1-11*
Let us contemplate, in this Mystery, how the Blessed Virgin Mary, when the time of the delivery was come, brought forth our Redeemer, Jesus Christ, at midnight, and laid Him in a manger, because there was no room for Him in the inns of Bethlehem.

Our Father. Hail Mary (10 times). Glory be.

Let us pray. O pure Mother of God, through thy virginal and most joyful delivery, whereby thou gavest to the world thine only Son, our Saviour, obtain for us, we beseech thee, through thine intercession, the grace to lead such pure and holy lives in this world that we may become worthy to sing, without ceasing, the mercies of thy Son, and His benefits to us by thee. Amen.

IV. The Presentation, *St. Luke 2:22-28*

Let us contemplate, in this Mystery, how the Blessed Virgin Mary, on the day of her Purification, presented the Child Jesus in the Temple, where holy Simeon, giving thanks to God, with great devotion received Him into his arms.

Our Father. Hail Mary (10 times). Glory be.

Let us pray. O holy Virgin, most admirable example and pattern of obedience, who didst present the Lord of the Temple in the Temple of God, obtain for us, of thy Blessed Son, that, with holy Simeon and devout Anna, we may praise and glorify Him forever. Amen.

V. The Finding in the Temple, *St. Luke 2:41-52*
Let us contemplate, in this Mystery, how the Blessed Virgin Mary, after having lost her beloved Son in Jerusalem, sought Him for the space of three days; and at length found Him in the Temple, sitting in the midst of the Doctors, hearing them, and asking them questions.

Our Father. Hail Mary (10 times). Glory be.

Let us pray. O most blessed Virgin, more than martyr in thy sufferings, and yet the comfort of such as are afflicted: by that unspeakable joy wherewith thy soul was filled when at length thou didst find thy dearly beloved Son, in the Temple, teaching in the midst of the Doctors, obtain of Him that we may so seek Him and find Him in His holy Orthodox Catholic Church as never more to be separated from Him. Amen.

The Sorrowful Mysteries
Said on Wednesdays, Fridays, and Sundays in Lent

I. The Agony in the Garden, *St. Luke 22:41-44*
Let us contemplate, in this Mystery, how our Lord Jesus was so afflicted for us in the Garden of Gethsemane that His Body was bathed in a bloody sweat, which ran down in great drops to the ground.

Our Father. Hail Mary (10 times). Glory be.

Let us pray. O holy Virgin, more than martyr, by that ardent prayer which our beloved Saviour poured forth to His Heavenly Father, vouchsafe to intercede for us, that, our passions being under the yoke of reason and faith, we may always, and in all things conform and subject ourselves to the holy will of God. Amen.

II. The Scourging, *St. Luke 23:13-16*
Let us contemplate, in this Mystery, how our Lord Jesus Christ was most cruelly scourged in the house of Pilate.

Our Father. Hail Mary (10 times). Glory be.

Let us pray. O Mother of God, Fountain of patience, through those stripes thy only and dearly beloved Son vouchsafed to suffer for us, obtain of Him for us grace to mortify our rebellious senses, to avoid the occasions of sin, and to be ready to suffer everything rather than offend God. Amen.

III. The Crowning with Thorns, *St. John 19:2-3*
Let us contemplate, in this Mystery, how those cruel ministers of Satan plaited a Crown of Thorns, and cruelly pressed it on the Sacred Head of our Lord Jesus Christ.

Our Father. Hail Mary (10 times). Glory be.

Let us pray. O Mother of our Eternal Prince, the King of Glory, by those sharp Thorns wherewith His Sacred Head was pierced, we beseech thee to obtain through thine intercession, that we may be delivered from all temptations of pride; and escape that shame which our sins deserve at the day of judgment. Amen.

IV. Carrying of the Cross, *St. John 19:17*
Let us contemplate, in this Mystery, how our Lord Jesus Christ, being sentenced to die bore, with most amazing patience, the Cross which was laid upon Him for His greater torment and ignominy.

Our Father. Hail Mary (10 times). Glory be.

Let us pray. O holy Virgin, model of patience, by the most painful carrying of the Cross, in which thy Son, our Lord Jesus Christ, bore the heavy weight of our sins, obtain for us of Him, through thine intercession, courage, and strength to follow His steps, and bear our cross after Him to the end of our lives. Amen.

V. The Crucifixion, *St. Mark 15:23-38*

Let us contemplate, in this Mystery, how our Lord Jesus Christ, being come to Golgotha, was stripped of His clothes, and His Hands and Feet were cruelly nailed to the Cross, in the presence of His most afflicted Mother.

Our Father. Hail Mary (10 times). Glory be.

Let us pray. O holy Mary, Mother of God, as the, Body of thy beloved Son was for us stretched upon the Cross, so may we offer up our souls and bodies to be crucified with Him, and our hearts to be pierced with grief at His most bitter Passion; and thou, O most sorrowful Mother, graciously vouchsafe to help us, by thy all-powerful prayers, to accomplish the work of our salvation. Amen.

The Glorious Mysteries
Said on Tuesdays, Saturdays, and Sundays from Pascha to Advent and then Christmas to Lent

I. The Resurrection, *St. Matthew 28:1-10*

Let us contemplate, in this Mystery, how our Lord Jesus Christ, triumphing gloriously over death, rose again the third day, immortal and impassible.

Our Father. Hail Mary (10 times). Glory be.

Let us pray. O glorious Virgin Mary, by that unspeakable joy thou didst receive in the Resurrection of thy divine Son, we beseech thee to obtain for us of Him that our hearts may never go astray after the false joys of this world, but may be wholly employed in seeking the true and solid joys of heaven. Amen.

II. The Ascension, *St. Luke 24:50-51*

Let us contemplate, in this Mystery, how our Lord Jesus Christ, forty days after His Resurrection, ascended into heaven, attended by Angels, in the sight of His most holy Mother and His holy Apostles and Disciples.

Our Father. Hail Mary (10 times). Glory be.

Let us pray. O Mother of God, consoler of the afflicted, as thy beloved Son, when He ascended into heaven, lifted up His hands and blessed his Apostles, as He departed from them; so vouchsafe, most holy Mother, to lift up thy pure hands to Him on our behalf, that we may enjoy the benefits of His blessing, and of thine, here on earth, and hereafter in heaven. Amen.

III. Pentecost, *Acts 1:13-14 and 2:1-4*

Let us contemplate, in this Mystery, how, our Lord Jesus Christ, being seated on the right hand of the Father, sent, as He had promised, the Holy Ghost upon His Apostles, who, after He had ascended, returned to Jerusalem, and continued in prayer and supplication, waiting for the fulfillment of His promise.

Our Father. Hail Mary (10 times). Glory be.

Let us pray. O Sacred Virgin, Tabernacle of the Holy Ghost, we beseech thee to obtain, by thine intercession, that this Comforter, whom thy beloved Son sent down upon His Apostles, filling them thereby with spiritual joy, may teach us in this world the true way of salvation, and make us walk in the way of virtue and good works. Amen.

IV. Assumption., *Apocalypse (Revelation) 22:1*
Let us contemplate, in this Mystery, how the glorious Virgin, several years after the Resurrection of her Son, passed out of this world unto Him, and was by Him taken into heaven, attended by the holy Angels.

Our Father. Hail Mary (10 times). Glory be.

Let us pray. O Holy Virgin, who, entering the heavenly mansions, didst fill the Angels with joy and man with hope: vouchsafe to intercede for us at the hour of our death, that, being delivered from the temptations and snares of the devil, we may joyfully pass out of this world to enjoy the happiness of eternal life. Amen.

V. Coronation, *Revelation 12:1 and 2 Timothy 4:8*

Let us contemplate, in this Mystery, how the glorious Virgin Mary was, to the great jubilation and exultation of the whole Heavenly Court, crowned by her Son with the brightest glory.

Our Father. Hail Mary (10 times). Glory be.

Let us pray. O glorious Queen of all the heavenly host, we beseech thee to accept these prayers, which, as a crown of roses, we offer at thy feet; and grant, most gracious Lady, that, by thy intercession, our souls may be so inflamed with the desire to see thee thus gloriously crowned, that it may never die within us until it is changed into the happy fruition of thy blessed sight. Amen.

The Memorare
(Which may be added to one's devotions as desired.)

Remember, O most gracious Virgin Mary, that never was it known that any one who fled to thy protection, implored thy help, and sought thy intercession, was left forsaken. Inspired with this confidence, I fly unto thee, O Virgin of virgins, my mother; to thee I come; before thee I stand, sinful and sorrowful. O Mother of the Word Incarnate, despise not my petitions, but in thy clemency hear and answer me. Amen.

STATIONS OF THE CROSS

O merciful Saviour, grant that while we follow Thy blessed footsteps along this Way of Sorrow, our hearts may be so touched with true contrition that Thou mayest turn our weeping into gladness by giving us remission of all our sins. Amen.

O most sorrowful Mother Mary, who first followed in the Way of the Cross, may the Most Adorable Trinity, through thy most powerful intercession, receive and accept, in reparation for our sins, and the sins of the whole world, the affections of sorrow and love, with which we intend, with God's help, to perform this holy exercise. Amen.

1. Jesus is Condemned to Death

℣. We adore Thee, O Christ, and we bless Thee.

℟. Because by Thy Holy Cross Thou hast redeemed the world.

Leaving the house of Caiaphas where He has been blasphemed, and the house of Herod where He has been mocked, Jesus is dragged before Pilate, His back torn with scourges, His head crowned with thorns; and He who on the last day will judge the living and the dead, is Himself condemned to a shameful death.

It was for us that Thou didst suffer, O blessed Jesus; it was for our sins Thou wast condemned to die. Oh, grant that we may detest them from the bottom of our hearts, and by this repentance obtain thy mercy and pardon.

O God, we love Thee with our whole hearts and above all things and are heartily sorry that we have offended Thee. May we never offend Thee any more. O may we love Thee without ceasing, and make it our delight to do in all things Thy most holy will.

Our Father...Hail, Mary...Amen.

℣. Have mercy upon us, O Lord.

℟. Have mercy upon us.

℣. May the souls of the faithful departed, through the mercy of God, rest in peace.

℟. Amen

>By the Cross sad vigil keeping,
>Stood the Mother, doleful weeping,
>Where her Son extended hung.

2.   Jesus Receives the Cross

℣.We adore Thee, O Christ, and we bless Thee.

℟. Because by Thy Holy Cross Thou hast redeemed the world.

A heavy cross is laid upon the bruised shoulders of Jesus. He receives it with meekness, nay with a secret joy, for it is the instrument with which He is to redeem the world. What efforts do we make, on the other hand, to escape all suffering as far as we can?

O Jesus, grant us, by virtue of Thy cross, to embrace with meekness and cheerful submission the difficulties of our state and to be ever ready to take up our cross and follow Thee.

O God, we love Thee with our whole hearts and above all things and are heartily sorry that we have offended Thee. May we never offend Thee any more. O may we love Thee without ceasing, and make it our delight to do in all things Thy most holy will.

Our Father...Hail, Mary...Amen.

℣. Have mercy upon us, O Lord.

℟. Have mercy upon us.

℣. May the souls of the faithful departed, through the mercy of God, rest in peace.

℟. Amen

> For her soul of joy bereaved,
> Smit with anguish, deeply grieved,
> Lo, the piercing sword hath wrung.

3. Jesus Falls the First Time

℣. We adore Thee, O Christ, and we bless Thee.

℟. Because by Thy Holy Cross Thou hast redeemed the world.

Bowing down under the weight of the Cross, Jesus, slowly sets forth on the way to Golgotha, amidst the mockeries and insults of the crowd. His agony in the garden has exhausted His body; He is sore with blows and wounds; His body fails Him, and He falls to the ground under the Cross.

O Jesus! who for out sins, Thou didst bear the heavy burden of the cross and fall under its weight, may the thought of Thy sufferings make us watchful over ourselves, and save us from any grievous fall into sin.

O God, we love Thee with our whole hearts and above all things and are heartily sorry that we have offended Thee. May we never offend Thee any more. O may we love Thee without ceasing, and make it our delight to do in all things Thy most holy will.

Our Father...Hail, Mary...Amen.

℣. Have mercy upon us, O Lord.

℟. Have mercy upon us.

℣. May the souls of the faithful departed, through the mercy of God, rest in peace.

℟. Amen

> Oh, how sad and sore distressed
> Now was she that Mother blessed
> Of the sole-begotten One!

4. Jesus Meets His Blessed Mother

℣. We adore Thee, O Christ, and we bless Thee.

℟. Because by Thy Holy Cross Thou hast redeemed the world.

Still burdened with His cross, and wounded yet more by his fall, Jesus proceeds on His Way. He is met by His all-holy Mother. What a meeting must that have been! What a sword must have pierced that Mother's bosom! What must have been the compassion of that Son for His holy Mother!

O Jesus! by the compassion which Thou didst feel for thy Mother, have compassion on us and give us a share in her intercession. O Mary, most sorrowful Mother! intercede for us, that through the sufferings of thy Son we may be delivered from everlasting death.

O God, we love Thee with our whole hearts and above all things and are heartily sorry that we have offended Thee. May we never offend Thee any more. O may we love Thee without ceasing, and make it our delight to do in all things Thy most holy will.

Our Father...Hail, Mary...Amen.

℣. Have mercy upon us, O Lord.

℟. Have mercy upon us.

℣. May the souls of the faithful departed, through the mercy of God, rest in peace.

℟. Amen

> Woe-begone with heart's prostration,
> Mother, meek, the bitter Passion
> Saw she of her glorious Son.

5. The Cross is Laid on Simon of Cyrene

℣. We adore Thee, O Christ, and we bless Thee.

℟. Because by Thy Holy Cross Thou hast redeemed the world.

As the strength of Jesus fails, and he is unable to proceed, the executioners seize and compel Simon of Cyrene to carry His cross. The virtue of that cross changes his heart, the compulsory task becomes a privilege and joy.

O Lord Jesus! may it be our privilege also to bear Thy cross; may we glory in nothing else; by it may the world be crucified unto us and we unto the world; may we never shrink from suffering, but rather rejoice if we be counted worthy to suffer for Thy Name's sake.

O God, we love Thee with our whole hearts and above all things and are heartily sorry that we have offended Thee. May we never offend Thee any more. O may we love Thee without ceasing, and make it our delight to do in all things Thy most holy will.

Our Father...Hail, Mary...Amen.

℣. Have mercy upon us, O Lord.

℟. Have mercy upon us.

℣. May the souls of the faithful departed, through the mercy of God, rest in peace.

℟. Amen

> Who on Christ's fond Mother looking,
> Such extreme affliction brooking,
> Born of woman, would not weep?

6. St. Veronica Wipes the Face of Jesus

℣. We adore Thee, O Christ, and we bless Thee.

℟. Because by Thy Holy Cross Thou hast redeemed the world.

As Jesus proceeds on the way, covered with the sweat of His Passion, a woman moved with compassion makes her way through the crowd and wipes His face with her veil. As a reward of her piety, the impression of His sacred countenance, the noble icon, is miraculously imprinted upon the veil.

O Jesus! may the contemplation of Thy long-suffering flood our eyes with tears of repentance, move us with the deepest compassion, make us to hate our sins; and kindle in our hearts more fervent love of Thee. May Thy most perfect image be graven in our mind, that we may be transformed into thy likeness.

O God, we love Thee with our whole hearts and above all things and are heartily sorry that we have offended Thee. May we never offend Thee any more. O may we love Thee without ceasing, and make it our delight to do in all things Thy most holy will.

Our Father...Hail, Mary...Amen.

℣. Have mercy upon us, O Lord.

℟. Have mercy upon us.

℣. May the souls of the faithful departed, through the mercy of God, rest in peace.

℟. Amen

> Who on Christ's fond Mother thinking,
> With her Son in sorrow sinking,
> Would not share her sorrows deep?

7.   Jesus Falls the Second Time

℣. We adore Thee, O Christ, and we bless Thee.

℟. Because by Thy Holy Cross Thou hast redeemed the world.

The pain of His wounds and the loss of blood increasing at every step of His way, again His strength fails Him and Jesus falls to the ground a second time. Our pride has caused His fall, it is our insolent haughtiness which crushes Him to the earth.

O Jesus! falling again under the burden of our sins, and of Thy sufferings for our sins, how often have we grieved Thee by our repeated falls into sin! Oh, may we rather die than offend Thee again!

O God, we love Thee with our whole hearts and above all things and are heartily sorry that we have offended Thee. May we never offend Thee any more. O may we love Thee without ceasing, and make it our delight to do in all things Thy most holy will.

Our Father...Hail, Mary...Amen.

℣. Have mercy upon us, O Lord.

℟. Have mercy upon us.

℣. May the souls of the faithful departed, through the mercy of God, rest in peace.

℟. Amen

For his People's sins rejected,
She her Jesus unprotected
Saw with thorns, with scourges rent.

8. The Women of Jerusalem Mourn for Jesus

℣. We adore Thee, O Christ, and we bless Thee.

℟. Because by Thy Holy Cross Thou hast redeemed the world.

At the sight of the sufferings of Jesus, some women in the crowd are so touched with sympathy, that they openly bewail and lament Him. Jesus knowing the things that were to come to pass, said, "Daughters of Jerusalem, weep not for Me, but weep for your children."

O Lord Jesus, we mourn and will mourn both for Thee and for ourselves, for Thy innocent sufferings and for our sins which caused them. Oh, teach us so to weep for our transgressions that we may be comforted, and escape those judgments prepared for all who reject Thee.

O God, we love Thee with our whole hearts and above all things and are heartily sorry that we have offended Thee. May we never offend Thee any more. O may we love Thee without ceasing, and make it our delight to do in all things Thy most holy will.

113

Our Father...Hail, Mary...Amen.

℣. Have mercy upon us, O Lord.

℟. Have mercy upon us.

℣. May the souls of the faithful departed, through the mercy of God, rest in peace.

℟. Amen

> Saw her Son from judgment taken,
> Her beloved in death forsaken,
> Till his Spirit forth he sent.

9. Jesus Falls the Third Time

℣. We adore Thee, O Christ, and we bless Thee.

℟. Because by Thy Holy Cross Thou hast redeemed the world.

Jesus has now arrived almost at the summit of Golgotha, but before He reaches the spot where He is to be crucified, His bodily strength again fails Him and He falls the third time, to be again dragged up and goaded onward by the brutal soldiery.

O Lord Jesus, we entreat Thee, by the merits of this Thy third most painful fall, to pardon our frequent relapses and our long continuance in sin; and may the thought of these Thy sufferings make us hate our sins more and more.

O God, we love Thee with our whole hearts and above all things and are heartily sorry that we have offended Thee. May we never offend Thee any more. O may we love Thee without ceasing, and make it our delight to do in all things Thy most holy will.

Our Father...Hail, Mary...Amen.

℣. Have mercy upon us, O Lord.

℞. Have mercy upon us.

℣. May the souls of the faithful departed, through the mercy of God, rest in peace.

℞. Amen

> Fount of love and holy sorrow,
> Mother, may my spirit borrow
> Somewhat of thy woe profound.

10. Jesus is Stripped of His Garments

℣. We adore Thee, O Christ, and we bless Thee.

℞. Because by Thy Holy Cross Thou hast redeemed the world.

Arrived at last at the place of sacrifice, the soldiers prepare to crucify Jesus, His garments are torn from His bleeding body, and He, the Holy of holies, stands exposed to the vulgar gaze of the rude and scoffing multitude.

O Lord Jesus, Thou didst endure this shame for our most shameful deeds. Strip us, we beseech Thee, of all false shame, conceit and pride, and make us so to humble ourselves voluntarily in this life, that we may escape everlasting shame in the world to come.

O God, we love Thee with our whole hearts and above all things and are heartily sorry that we have offended Thee. May we never offend Thee any more. O may we love Thee without ceasing, and make it our delight to do in all things Thy most holy will.

Our Father...Hail, Mary...Amen.

℣. Have mercy upon us, O Lord.

℟. Have mercy upon us.

℣. May the souls of the faithful departed, through the mercy of God, rest in peace.

℟. Amen

> Unto Christ with pure emotion
> May I raise my heart's devotion,
>   Love to read in every wound.

11. Jesus is Nailed to the Cross
℣. We adore Thee, O Christ, and we bless Thee.

℟. Because by Thy Holy Cross Thou hast redeemed the world.

The cross is laid upon the ground and Jesus is stretched, out upon His bed of death. At one and the same time He offers His bruised limbs to His heavenly Father in behalf of fallen man, and to His fierce executioners to be nailed by them to the shameful cross. The blows are struck! The Precious Blood streams forth!

O Jesus! nailed to the cross, fasten our hearts there also, that they may be united to thee until death shall strike us with its fatal blow, and with our last breath we shall have yielded up our souls to Thee.

O God, we love Thee with our whole hearts and above all things and are heartily sorry that we have offended Thee. May we never offend Thee any more. O may we love Thee without ceasing, and make it our delight to do in all things Thy most holy will.

Our Father...Hail, Mary...Amen.

℣. Have mercy upon us, O Lord.

℟. Have mercy upon us.

℣. May the souls of the faithful departed, through the mercy of God, rest in peace.

℟. Amen

Those five wounds of Jesus smitten,
Mother! in my heart be written,
Deep as in thine own they be.

12. Jesus Dies upon the Cross

℣. We adore Thee, O Christ, and we bless Thee.

℟. Because by Thy Holy Cross Thou hast redeemed the world.

For three hours Jesus has hung upon His pierced hands; His blood has run down in streams; and in the midst of excruciating sufferings, He has pardoned His murderers, promised the bliss of Paradise to the good thief, and committed His blessed Mother and Beloved Disciple to each other's care. All is now finished; and meekly bowing down His head, He gives up His spirit.

O Jesus! we devoutly embrace that honored cross where Thou didst love us even unto death. In that death we place all our confidence. Henceforth let us live only for Thee; and in dying for Thee let us die loving Thee.

O God, we love Thee with our whole hearts and above all things and are heartily sorry that we have offended Thee. May we never offend Thee any more. O may we love Thee without ceasing, and make it our delight to do in all things Thy most holy will.

Our Father...Hail, Mary...Amen.

℣. Have mercy upon us, O Lord.

℟. Have mercy upon us.

℣. May the souls of the faithful departed, through the mercy of God, rest in peace.

℟. Amen

> Thou, my Saviour's Cross who bearest,
>   Thou, thy Son's rebuke who sharest,
>   Let me share them both with thee.

13. Jesus is Taken Down from the Cross
℣. We adore Thee, O Christ, and we bless Thee.

℟. Because by Thy Holy Cross Thou hast redeemed the world.

The great crowds have left the heights of Golgotha and few remain save the beloved Disciple and the holy women, who at the foot of the Cross are striving to stem the grief of Christ's most loving Mother. Joseph of Arimathea and Nicodemus take the body of her Divine Son from the cross and deposit it in her arms.

O Mary, most blessed Theotokos, thou bearest in thine arms thine only Son, now dead, who often rested His head, in sleep upon thy breast. Pray for us, that, as thou holdest Him lifeless in death, He may bear us up in the hour of our death in His everlasting arms.

119

O God, we love Thee with our whole hearts and above all things and are heartily sorry that we have offended Thee. May we never offend Thee any more. O may we love Thee without ceasing, and make it our delight to do in all things Thy most holy will.

Our Father...Hail, Mary...Amen.

℣. Have mercy upon us, O Lord.

℟. Have mercy upon us.

℣. May the souls of the faithful departed, through the mercy of God, rest in peace.

℟. Amen

> Mine with thee be that sad station,
> There to watch the great Salvation,
> Wrought upon the atoning tree.

14. Jesus is Laid in the Tomb

℣. We adore Thee, O Christ, and we bless Thee.

℟. Because by Thy Holy Cross Thou hast redeemed the world.

The body of her dearly beloved Son is taken from His Mother, and laid by the disciples in the tomb. The tomb is closed and there the lifeless body remains until the hour of its glorious resurrection

We too, O God, will descend into the grave whenever it shall please Thee, as it shall please Thee, and wheresoever it shall please Thee. Suffer our sinful bodies to return to their parent dust; but do Thou, in Thy great mercy, receive our immortal souls, and when our bodies have risen again place them likewise in thy kingdom, and that we may love, glorify, and bless Thy holy Name, now and for ever and ever. Amen.

O God, we love Thee with our whole hearts and above all things and are heartily sorry that we have offended Thee. May we never offend Thee any more. O may we love Thee without ceasing, and make it our delight to do in all things Thy most holy will.

Our Father...Hail, Mary...Amen.

℣. Have mercy upon us, O Lord.

℟. Have mercy upon us.

℣. May the souls of the faithful departed, through the mercy of God, rest in peace.

℟. Amen

To my parting soul be given
Entrance at the gate of Heaven,
And in Paradise a place.

Conclusion

Our Father...Hail Mary...

Antiphon. Christ became obedient unto death for us, even the death of the Cross.

Let us pray. Almighty God, we beseech Thee graciously to behold this Thy family for which our Lord Jesus Christ was contented to be betrayed, and given up into the hands of wicked men, and to suffer death upon the Cross. Through Jesus Christ our Lord, who liveth and reigneth with thee in the unity of the Holy Ghost, God, world without end. Amen. *Repeat Antiphon.*

NOVENA IN PREPARATION FOR CHRISTMAS

Daily Opening: O Lord Jesus Christ, who for our sake didst vouchsafe to descend from Thy throne of glory to this vale of tears and woe; who wast conceived by the Holy Ghost, born of the Virgin Mary, and was made Man; make, we beseech, Thee, our hearts a fit habitation for Thyself. Beautify and fill them with all spiritual graces, and possess them wholly by Thy power. Give us grace to prepare for Thy coming with deep humility, to receive Thee with burning love, and to hold Thee fast with a firm faith; that we may never leave Thee nor forsake Thee, who livest and reignest, world without end. Amen.

Antiphon of the Day

December 16: O Shepherd that rulest Israel, Thou that leadest Joseph like a sheep, come to guide and comfort us.

December 17: O Wisdom that comest out of the mouth of the Most High, that reachest from one end to another, and orderest all things mightily and sweetly, come to teach us the way of prudence.

December 18: O Adonai, and Ruler of the house of Israel, Who didst appear unto Moses in the burning bush, and gavest him the law in Sinai, come to redeem us with an outstretched arm!

December 19: O Root of Jesse, which standest for an ensign of the people, at Whom the kings shall shut their mouths, Whom the Gentiles shall seek, come to deliver us, do not tarry.

December 20: O Key of David, and Sceptre of the house of Israel, that openeth and no man shutteth, and shutteth and no man openeth, come to liberate the prisoner from the prison, and them that sit in darkness, and in the shadow of death.

December 21: O Dayspring, Brightness of the everlasting ight, Son of justice, come to give light to them that sit in darkness and in the shadow of death!

December 22: O King of Gentiles, yea, and desire thereof! O Corner-stone, that makest of two one, come to save man, whom Thou hast made out of the dust of the earth!

December 23: O Emmanuel, our King and our Law-giver, Longing of the Gentiles, yea, and salvation thereof, come to save us, O Lord our God!

December 24: O Thou that sittest upon the cherubim, God of hosts, come, show Thy face, and we shall be saved.

Daily Conclusion: Our Father. Hail, Mary. Glory be.

O Merciful Jesus, who didst in Thy early infancy commence Thy office of Saviour by shedding, Thy precious Blood and assuming for us that name which is above all names; we, thank Thee for such early proofs of Thy infinite love. We venerate Thy sacred name in union with the profound respect of the angel who first announced it to the earth and unite our affections to the sentiments of tender devotion which the adorable name of Jesus has in all ages enkindled in the hearts of Thy saints.

Animated with a firm faith in Thy unerring word, and penetrated with confidence in Thy mercy, we now humbly remind Thee of the promise Thou hast made, that where two or three should assemble in Thy Name, Thou Thyself wouldst be in the midst of them. Come, then, into the midst of us, most amiable Jesus, for it is in Thy sacred Name we are here assembled; come into our hearts, that we may be governed by Thy holy Ghost; mercifully grant us, through that adorable Name, which is the joy of heaven, the terror of hell, the consolation of the afflicted and the solid ground of our unlimited confidence, all the petitions we make in this novena.

O blessed Mother of our Redeemer, who didst participate so sensibly in the sufferings of thy dear Son when He shed His sacred Blood and assumed for us the name of Jesus, obtain for us, through that adorable Name, the favours we petition in this novena.

Beg also, that the most ardent love may imprint on our hearts that sacred Name, that it may be always in our minds and frequently on our lips; that it may be our defense and our refuge in the temptations and trials of life, and our consolation and support in the hour-of death. Amen.

NOVENA IN PREPARATION FOR PENTECOST

Daily Opening: In the Name of the Father, and of the Son, arid of the Holy Ghost. Amen.
V: Come, O Holy Ghost, Come:

℟. And fill us with Thy heavenly flame.

Antiphon of the Day

1st Day: Come, O Holy Ghost, the Lord and Life-giver, take up Thy dwelling within my soul, and make of it Thy sacred temple. Make me live by grace as an adopted son of God. Pervade all the energies of my soul, and created in me a fountain of living water springing up into life everlasting.

2nd Day: Come, O Spirit of Wisdom, and reveal to my soul the mysteries of heavenly things, their exceeding greatness, and power, and beauty. Teach me to love them above and beyond all the passing joys and satisfactions of earth. Show me the way by which I may be able to attain to them, and possess them, and hold them hereafter, my own forever.

3rd Day: Come, O Spirit of Understanding, and enlighten our minds, that we may know and believe all the mysteries of salvation, and may merit at last to see the eternal light in Thy light; and in the light of glory to have the clear vision of Thee and the Father and the Son.

4th Day: Come, O Spirit of Counsel, help and guide me in all my ways, that I may always do Thy holy will. Incline my heart to that which is good, turn it away from all that is evil, and direct me by the path of Thy

Commandments to the goal of eternal life for which I long.

5th Day: Come, O Spirit of Fortitude, and give fortitude to our souls. Make our hearts strong in all trials and in all distress, pouring forth abundantly into them the gifts of strength, that we may be able to resist the attacks of the devil.

6th Day: Come, O Spirit of Knowledge and make us understand and despise the emptiness and nothingness of the World. Give us grace to use the world only for Thy glory and the salvation of Thy creatures. May we Always be very faithful in putting Thy rewards before every earthly gift.

7th Day: Come, O Spirit of Piety, possess my heart; incline it to a true faith in Thee, to a holy love of Thee, my God, that with my whole soul I may seek Thee, and find Thee my best, my truest joy.

8th Day: Come, O Spirit of holy Feat, penetrate my inmost heart, that I may set Thee, my Lord and God, before my face forever; and shun all things that can offend Thee, so that I may be made worthy to appear before the pure eyes of Thy divine Majesty in the heaven of heavens, where Thou livest and reignest in unity of the Ever-blessed Trinity, God, world without end.

9th Day: Come, O Holy Comforter, and grant us a relish for heavenly things. Produce in our souls the flowers and fruit of virtue, so that, being filled with all sweetness and joy in the pursuit of good, we may attain unto eternal blessedness.

Daily Conclusion: Our Father. Hail, Mary. Glory be.

O Holy Ghost, my Lord and my God, I adore Thee and humbly acknowledge here in Thy sacred presence that I am nothing, and can do nothing, without, Thy operation within me. Come, great Paraclete, Thou Father of the poor, Thou Comforter the blest, fulfill the promise of our Saviour, who would not leave us orphans, and enter my mind and heart as Thou didst descend on the day of Pentecost upon Thy holy Mother of Jesus and upon His first disciples. Grant that I may have a part in those gifts which Thou didst so prodigally bestow upon them.

Take from my heart all that is not pleasing to Thee and make of it a worthy dwelling place for Jesus.

Illumine my mind, that I may see and understand the things that are for my eternal welfare.

Inflame my heart with pure love of the Father, that, cleansed from attachment to all unworthy objects, my whole life may be hidden with Jesus in God.

Strengthen my will, that it may be conformable to the will of my Creator and guided by Thy holy inspirations.

Aid me to practice the heavenly virtues of humility, poverty and obedience which are taught to me in the earthly life of Jesus.

Descend upon me, O mighty Ghost, that, inspired and encouraged by Thee, I may faithfully fulfill the duties of my state in life, carry my daily cross with patience and courage, and accomplish the Fathers will for me perfectly. Make me, day by day, more holy and give to me that heavenly peace which the world cannot give.

O Holy Ghost, thou Giver of every good and perfect gift, grant to me the intentions of this novena prayer. May the Father's will be done in me and through me. And mayest Thou, O mighty Ghost of the living God, be praised and glorified for ever and ever. Amen.

NOVENA TO THE BLESSED VIRGIN MARY

Said Daily for Nine Days

In the Name of the Father, and of the Son, and of the Holy Ghost. Amen.

V. The Angel declared unto Mary:

R. And she conceived of the Holy Ghost.

Our Father. Hail, Mary. Glory be.

Mary, Virgin ever blessed! who can worthily praise thee or give thee thanks, who, by that wondrous assent of thy will, didst rescue a fallen world? What honours can the weakness of our human nature pay to thee, which by thy intervention alone has found the way to restoration? Accept, then, such poor thanks as we have here to offer, though they are unequal to thy merits; and, receiving our vows obtain by thy prayers the remission of our offenses. Carry thou our prayers within the sanctuary of the heavenly audience, and bring forth from it the medicine of our reconciliation. Through thee may those sins become pardonable the release from which through thee we ask of God, and that be granted which we demand with confidence.

Accept what we offer, grant us what we seek, spare us what we fear, for thou art the sole hope of sinners. Through thee we hope for the forgiveness of our faults and in thee, most blessed Virgin, is the hope of our reward. Holy Mary, succour the wretched, help the faint-hearted, comfort the sorrowful, pray for the people, shield the clergy, intercede for all women consecrated to God, let all feel thine aid. who keep thy holy commemoration. Be thou at hand, ready to aid our prayers, when we pray, and bring back to us that answer we desire.

Make it thy care to intercede ever for the people of God – thou who, blessed of God, didst merit to bear the Redeemer of the world who liveth and reigneth forever and ever. Amen.

NOVENA FOR ONE DEPARTED

Daily Opening: In the Name of the Father, and of the Son, and of the Holy Ghost. Amen.

℣: May the souls of the faithful, departed. rest in peace.

℞. And may perpetual light shine upon them.

Prayer of the Day

1st Day: O God, whose nature and property is forever to have mercy and to forgive, receive our humble petitions for the soul of Thy servant N., which Thou hast commanded to depart out of this world: deliver *him* not into the hand of the enemy, neither forsake *him* at the last; but command *him* to be received by Thy holy Angels, and brought to the country of Paradise; that forasmuch as *he* hoped and believed in Thee, *he* may not undergo the pains of hell, but be made partaker of everlasting felicity. Through Jesus Christ our Lord. Amen.

2nd Day: To Thee, O Lord, I commend the soul of Thy servant N., that being dead to the world, *he* may live to Thee; and whatsoever sins *he* hath committed, through the frailty of *his* mortal nature, do Thou wash away by the pardon of Thy most merciful loving-kindness. Through Jesus Christ our Lord. Amen.

3rd Day: O God, whose mercies cannot be numbered; accept my prayers on behalf of the soul of Thy servant N. departed this life, and grant *him* an entrance into the land of light and joy, in the fellowship of Thy Saints Through Jesus Christ Our Lord. Amen.

4th Day: Incline Thine ear, O Lord, unto the prayers wherewith I humbly, entreat Thy mercy: that the soul of Thy servant, which Thou hast bidden to depart this life, may by Thee be set in the abode of peace and light, and made partaker of the fellowship of Thine elect. Through Jesus Christ our Lord. Amen.

5th Day: Absolve, O Lord, I pray Thee, the soul Thy servant N., from every bond of sin: that at the general Resurrection at the last day *he* may find refreshment in the of Thy Saints. Through Jesus Christ our Lord. Amen.

6th Day: I beseech Thee, O Lord, of Thy loving kindness have mercy upon the soul of Thy servant N., and now that *he* is released from the contagion of mortality, do Thou restore *his* portion in everlasting salvation. Through Jesus Christ our Lord. Amen.

7th Day: I implore. Thee, O Lord, mercifully to grant companionship with the blessed in heaven to soul of Thy servant N., whose death I commemorate. Through Jesus Christ our Lord. Amen.

8th Day: Accept, O Lord, I pray Thee, the prayers which I humbly offer unto Thee for the soul of Thy servant N., beseeching Thee to grant that, whatever defilements *he* may have contracted in *his* conversation in this life being pardoned by Thy goodness, *he* may be made partaker of those unspeakable joys that Thou hast prepared for Thine elect. Through Jesus Christ our Lord. Amen.

9th Day: Grant, O Lord, this mercy to Thy servant departed, who desired to do Thy will, that *he* may not receive the punishment of *his* misdeeds: and that, as true faith joined *him* to the company of the faithful here below, so Thy mercy may bring *him* to the Angelic company of heaven. Through Jesus Christ our Lord. Amen.

Daily Conclusion: Our Father. Hail, Mary. Glory be.

℣. Rest eternal grant unto them, O Lord.

℟. And let perpetual light shine upon them.

℣. May they rest in peace.

133

℟. Amen.

BENEDICTION

O Salutaris Hostia
O SAVING Victim opening wide
The Gate of Heaven to man below,
Our foes press on from every side,
Thine aid supply, Thy strength bestow.
All praise and thanks to Thee ascend
For evermore, blest One in Three;
O grant us life that shall not end,
In our true native land with Thee. Amen.

Tantum Ergo
THEREFORE we, before him bending,
This great Sacrament revere;
Types and shadows have their ending,
For the newer rite is here;
Faith, our outward sense befriending,
Makes the inward vision clear.
To the everlasting Father,
And the Son who reigns on high
With the Holy Ghost proceeding
Forth with One eternally,
Be salvation, honor, blessing,
Might and endless majesty. Amen.

P. Thou gavest them bread from heaven.

℟. Containing within itself all sweetness.

P. Let us pray. O God, who in this wonderful Sacrament has left us a perpetual Memorial of Thy Passion: Grant us, we beseech Thee, so to venerate the Sacred Mysteries of Thy Body and Blood; that we may ever perceive within ourselves the fruit of Thy redemption; who with the Father in the unity of the Holy Ghost, livest and reignest God, world without end.

℟. Amen

℟: *Repeat the priest*

P. Blessed be God.
Blessed be His Holy Name.
Blessed be Jesus Christ, true God and true Man.
Blessed be the Name of Jesus.
Blessed be His most Sacred Heart.
Blessed be Jesus in the Most Holy Sacrament of the Altar.
Blessed be the Great Mother of God, Mary most Holy.
Blessed be the name of Mary, Virgin and Mother.
Blessed be Saint Joseph, her most chaste spouse.
Blessed be God in His Angels and in His Saints.

Antiphon: Let us forever adore, the Most Holy Sacrament.

O praise the Lord, all ye • nations; * praise him, • all
ye people.

For His merciful kindness is ever more and more •
toward us; * and the truth of the Lord endureth for •
ever. Praise the Lord.

Glory be to the Father • and to the Son, * and • to
the Holy Ghost.

As it was in the beginning, † is now, and ev- • er shall
be, * world • without end. Amen. *The Antiphon is
repeated.*

Part 5

Confession & Preparation

EXAMINATION OF CONSCIENCE

Preliminary Examination

When did you make your last confession? Did you have real sorrow for the sins then told? Did you conceal or forget any grievous sin? Have you performed your penance, and done as your confessor directed? Have you really tried to keep your good resolutions?

Invocation of the Holy Ghost

O Holy Ghost, Source of all light, Spirit of wisdom, of understanding, and of knowledge, come to my assistance and enable me to make a good confession. Enlighten me, and help me now to know my sins as one day I shall be forced to recognize them before Thy judgment seat. Bring to my mind the evil which I have done and the good which I have neglected. Permit me not to be blinded by self-love. Grant me, moreover, heartfelt sorrow for my transgressions, and the grace of a sincere confession, so that I may be forgiven and admitted to Thy friendship. Amen.

THE SEVEN GRIEVOUS SINS (The Passions)

I. PRIDE. *Pride is putting self in the place of God as the center and objective of our life. It is the refusal to recognize our status as created, dependent on God, who is uncreated, for our existence and placed by him in a specific relationship to the rest of his creation.*

Irreverence. Have you deliberately neglected the worship of God on Sunday in his Church? Were you content with just "going through the motions" when you were at church? Have you disregarded Holy Days and additional opportunities for worshipping God? Have you failed to thank God or to adequately express your gratitude to God for all the many blessings he gives you every day?

Have you shown disrespect of God or holy things by deliberately treating them, in thought, word, or deed, in a profane, contemptuous or over-familiar manner? Have you used holy things for personal advantage? Have you attempted to bribe or placate God by religious practices or promises?

Sentimentality. Have you been satisfied with pious feelings and beautiful ceremonies without striving to obey God's will?

Presumption. Have you been dependent on yourself rather than on God, with the consequent negligence of the sacraments and prayer? Have you dispensed yourself from ordinary duties on the grounds that you are too superior for those duties or obligations? Have you been satisfied or complacent over your spiritual achievements? Have you refused to avoid, when possible, immediate temptation? Have you preferred your own schemes or techniques to those of the

Church? Have you held to or encouraged foolish optimism?

Have you failed to recognize your job as a divine vocation, or to offer your work to God? Have you unwilling to surrender to and abide in Christ, to let him act in and through you? Have you failed to offer intercessions for persons or causes that have, or should have, your interest and support, to God?

Distrust. Have you refused to recognize God's wisdom, providence and love? Have you been worried, anxious, had misgivings, or scrupulosity? Have you been guided by your own perfectionism rather than by the love of God? Have you attempted to discern or control the future by spiritualism, astrology, fortune-telling or the like? Have you practiced magic or superstition?

Over-sensitiveness. Have you expected that others will dislike, reject or mistreat you? Have you been over-ready to interpret the attitude of others, or quick to take offense? Have you held to unfounded suspicions?

Have you been timid in accepting responsibility, or been cowardly in facing difficulty or suffering? Have you surrendered yourself to feelings of depression, gloom, pessimism, discouragement, self-pity, or fear of death, instead of fighting to be brave, cheerful and hopeful?

Disobedience. Have you rejected God's known will in favor of your own interests or pleasures? Have you been disobedient to the legitimate (and therefore divinely ordained) laws, regulations or authority of the Church, state, husband, parents, teachers, etc.? Have you been slow and reluctant to give your obedience to such authority? Have you failed, when in authority, to fulfill responsibilities or to consider the best interests of those under you?

Have you refused to learn God's will as revealed in Scripture, expounded in instructions or expert advice, or discernible through prayer, meditation or the reading of religious books? Have you been absorbed in your own affairs, leaving little time, energy or interest for the things of God?

Have you violated the confidence of someone? Have you broken legitimate promises or contracts? Have you done so through irresponsibility or through treachery (willfulness and malice)? Have you unnecessarily disappointed another, or caused shame or anxiety to those who love you?

Impenitence. Have you refused to search out and face up to your sins, or to confess and admit them before God? Have you disregarded your sins or held to the pretense that you are better than truly you are? Have you justified yourself or discounted your sins as being insignificant, normal or inevitable? Have you been self-righteous in comparing yourself with others?

Have you refused to accept just punishment or to make due reparation for your words and deeds when possible? Have you resorted to deceit or lying to escape the consequences of your sins? Have you allowed another to suffer the blame for your faults? Have you tried to overcompensate or attempted self-reform or self-vengeance, to avoid surrendering to God in humble penitence?

Have you felt shame (hurt pride) or sorrow for yourself because your sins make you less respectable than you like to think you are, or because you fear punishment or injury to your reputation, rather than feeling sorrow for what sin is in the eyes of God? Have you refused to admit you were in the wrong or to apologize? Have you refused to accept forgiveness from God or others? Have you doubted that God can forgive your sins or failed to make your confession when you need to do so? Have you been unwilling to forgive yourself?

Vanity. Have you taken the credit, rather than giving credit and glory to God, for your talents, abilities, insights, accomplishments and/or good works? Have you refused to admit indebtedness to others, or adequately to express gratitude for their help? Have you been a hypocrite? Have you held pretense to virtues you do, not possess? Have you feigned humility, when you really were not humble? Have you harshly judged others for faults you excuse in yourself?

Have you boasted, exaggerated, drawn attention to yourself by talking too much, by claiming ability, wisdom, experience or influence you do not have, or by eccentric or ostentatious behavior? Have you held undue concern over, or expenditure of, time or money? Have you spent too much energy on your appearance, looks, dress, surroundings, etc., to impress others? Have you deliberately been slovenly for the same purpose? Have you sought, desired or relished flattery or compliments?

Arrogance. Have you insisted that others conform to your wishes, recognize your leadership, or accept your own estimation of your worth? Have you been overbearing, argumentative, opinionated, or obstinate?

Snobbery. Have you had pride over your race, family, position, personality, education, skill, achievements, or possessions?

II. ANGER. *Anger is open rebellion against God or our fellow creatures. Its purpose and desire is to eliminate any obstacle to our self-seeking, to retaliate*

143

against any threat to our security, and to avenge any personal insult or injury. It is only appropriate to have anger towards sin or the evil one, not towards a human.

Resentment. Have you refused to discern, accept or fulfill God's vocation for you? Have you been dissatisfied with the talents, abilities or opportunities God has given you? Have you been unwilling to face up to difficulties or sacrifices? Have you unjustly rebelled or complained about the circumstances of your life? Have you tried to escape from reality or attempted to force your will upon reality? Have you indulged yourself in daydreams to escape reality? Have you transferred blame for your maladjustment to God, to your parents, to society, or to other individuals? Have you had hatred for God, or been antisocial? Have you been cynical? Have you harbored annoyance at the contrariness of things? Have you used profanity or grumbled at reality?

Pugnacity. Have you attacked another in anger? Have you committed murder or desire to? Have you been combative or nursed grudges? Have you injured another person by striking, cursing or insulting him? Have you injured another person by damaging his reputation or property? Have you been quarrelsome; bickered with, contradicted, nagged, been rude to, or snubbed others?

Retaliation. Have you wrought your vengeance for wrongs, real or imagined, or plotted vengeance? Have you been harsh or excessive in punishing those for whom you are responsible? Have you been hostile, sullen or exercised rash judgment? Have you refused to forgive, or to offer or accept reconciliation? Have you been unwilling to love, to do good to, or to pray for your enemies? Have you boycotted or ostracized another for selfish reasons? Have you spoiled the pleasure of others by being uncooperative or filled with disdain, because you have not gotten your way, or because you feel out of sorts or superior?

III. ENVY. *Envy is dissatisfaction with our place in God's order of creation, manifested in begrudging his gifts and vocation to others.*

Jealousy. Have you taken offense at the talents, success or good fortune of others? Have you been selfish or unnecessarily competitive? Have you taken pleasure at the difficulty or distress of others? Have you belittled others?

Malice. Have you felt ill will towards another or dealt in false accusations, slander, or backbiting? Have you read false motives into others behavior? Have you initiated, collected or retold gossip? Have you aroused, fostered or organized antagonism against others? Have you been unnecessarily critical, even when you've related the truth? Have you deliberately annoyed others, or teased or bullied them?

Contempt. Have you scorned another's virtue, ability, shortcomings, or failings? Have you felt prejudice against those you consider inferior, or who consider you inferior, if who seem to threaten your security or position? Have you ridiculed anyone, institutions, or ideals?

IV. COVETOUSNESS. *Covetousness is the refusal to respect the integrity of other creatures, expressed in the inordinate accumulation of material things; in the use of other people for our personal advantage; or in the quest for status, power or security at their expense.*

Ambition. Have you pursued status, power, influence, reputation, or possessions at the expense of moral law, of other obligations, or of the rights of others? Have you been ruthless or unfair in competition? Have you put yourself or your family first? Have you conformed to standards you recognize as wrong or inadequate to get ahead? Have participated in intrigue or conspiracy for self-advancement?

Domination. Have you sought to use or possess others? Have you been over-protective of your children? Have you refused to correct or punish your children lest you lose their affection? Have you insisted that they conform to your ideal for them

146

contrary to their own vocation? Have you imposed your will on others by force, guile, whining, or refusal to cooperate? Have you been over-ready to advise or command? Have you abused authority? Have you patronized, pauperized, or put others under a debt of gratitude? Have you considered yourself ill-used when others' affection or compliance is not for sale?

Have you been a sycophant (attempted to win favor, support, affection or advancement in position, through practicing flattery of persons of influence)? Have you refused to uphold the truth, to fulfill your duties, to perform good works, or to defend those wrongfully attacked because you fear criticism or ridicule, or because you seek to gain the favor and approval of others? Have you lead, tempted, or encouraged another to sin?

Avarice. Have you inordinately pursued wealth or material things? Have you stolen, been dishonest, misrepresented, or shared in stolen goods? Have you Cheated in business, taxes, school or games? Have you made worldly success the goal of your life or the standard for judging others?

Prodigality. Have you wasted natural resources or your personal possessions? Have you been extravagant or lived beyond your income, to impress others or to maintain status? Have you failed to pay debts you acquired? Have you gambled more than you could afford to lose, or to win unearned profits? Have you unnecessarily borrowed or been careless with others' money? Have you spent on yourself what is needed for the welfare of others?

Penuriousness. Have you been unduly protective of wealth or security? Have you selfishly insisted on vested interests or on claimed rights? Have you refused to support or to help those who have a claim on you? Have you "sponged on others?" Have you been stingy? Have you failed to give the due proportion of your income to the Church and charity, or of your time and energy to good works? Have you failed to pay pledges promised to the Church or charities when you have been able to do so?

V. GLUTTONY. *Gluttony is the overindulgence of food and drink, and by extension the inordinate quest for pleasure or comfort.*

Intemperance. Have you been overindulgent in food, drink, smoking, or other physical pleasures? Have you been fastidious, fussy, demanded excessively high standards, or been a dilettante? Have you condemned some material things or pleasures as evil in themselves, attempting to prohibit their use rather than their abuse?

Lack of Discipline. Have you been negligent in keeping to the Church's days and seasons of fasting?

Have you failed to use other needed means of self-discipline? Have you neglected your bodily health—not getting sufficient rest, recreation, exercise, or wholesome nourishment? Have you failed to use or to cooperate with available medical care when ill? Have you used sickness to escape responsibilities?

VI. LUST. *Lust is the misuse of sex for personal gratification, debasing it from the holy purpose for which God has given it to us.*

Unchastity. Have you violated the Church's marriage laws? Have you lacked consideration for your spouse in partaking of the marital relationship? Have you refused to fulfill the purpose of Holy Matrimony in the bringing forth and giving adequate care of children, or to take your full share in the responsibilities or work involved? Have you been unfaithful to your spouse? Have you indulged in sexual contact outside of matrimony, in thought or act, alone or with others? Have I viewed immoral material or content, or delighted in inappropriate images in any way?

Immodesty. Have you stimulated sexual desire in others by words, dress, or actions; or in yourself by reading, pictures, or fantasies? Have you collected or recounted sexual stories?

Prudery. Have you had a fear of sex or condemned it as evil, even when sanctified within marriage? Have you refused to seek instruction from the Church regarding a true understanding of sexuality, or attempted to prevent others from obtaining it? Have you stimulated excessive and harmful curiosity by undue secrecy?

Cruelty. Have you deliberately inflicted pain, mental or physical, on another. Have you tormented or abused animals?

VII. SLOTH. *Sloth is the refusal to respond to our opportunities for growth, service or sacrifice.*

Laziness. Have you been indolent in performing spiritual, mental or physical duties? Have you neglected your family, business or social obligations? Have you been discourteous because you didn't wish to spend the extra energy? Have you procrastinated in performing disliked tasks? Have you involved yourself in busy-ness or triviality to avoid more important commitments? Have you devoted excessive time to rest, recreation, amusement, television, light reading or the like? Have you wasted your employer's time, or performed shoddy or inadequate work?

Indifference. Have you been unconcerned over injustice to others, especially that caused by currently accepted social standards? Have you been unmindful of the suffering of those around you? Have you failed to become adequately informed on the Christian principles involved in contemporary issues? Have you neglected duties to state or community? Have you failed to provide adequately for those whom you employ, or to treat them justly? Have you required them to stay late to perform urgent tasks, and then forced them to "lose" the overtime they had acquired for the work required by you?

Have you ignored the needy, lonely or unpopular people in your own family, or in the parish family, or in the neighborhood? Have you been unwilling to minister to them? Have you been insufficiently attentive to the religious and other needs of your family? Have you failed to fulfill your obligation of Christian missionary witness?

PRAYERS FOR CONTRITION

1. Consider the sins which have come to your remembrance, placing them and their circumstances before you, as distinctly as you can.
2. Consider, **WHO GOD IS**, against whom you have sinned, how great, how good, how gracious to you; that He made you, that He gave His Only Son to die for you, that He made you His child in Baptism, that He has loaded you with blessings and prepared heaven for you. Consider how patient He has been with you—how long-suffering in calling you and moving you to repent.
3. Consider the infinite wickedness of sin.

4.   Consider the consequences of one grave sin: that you might justly now be banished from God's presence for ever for one single unrepented, deadly sin; how many have you committed!

O my God, I cry unto Thee with the prodigal: Father, I have sinned against heaven and before Thee, and am no more worthy to be called Thy son.

I have gone astray like a sheep that is lost. O seek Thy servant, for I have not forgotten Thy commandments.

Enter not into judgment with Thy servant, O Lord. O spare me for Thy mercy's sake.

Prove me, O God, and know my heart; examine me, and know my paths.

Thou whose property is always to have mercy and to spare, O meet me in pity, embrace me in love, and forgive me all my sin.

I confess my sins unto Thee, O Christ, Healer of our souls, O Lord of Life. Heal me, heal me of my spiritual sickness, Thou who art long-suffering and of tender mercy; heal me, O Lord Christ.

Accept my supplications, O Thou Holy Ghost, unto whom every heart is open, every desire known, and from whom no secret is hid, and who givest life to our souls; hear and answer, O Spirit of God.

O Heavenly Father, who willest not that any sinner should perish, give me true repentance for this my sin, that I perish not!

To what misery am I come by my own fault! O merciful God, pity and forgive me for Jesus' sake.

Thine eyes, O God, are as a flame of fire searching my inmost heart. O pardon my sin, for it is great!

Thou, God, seest me in all the foulness of my sins! Blessed Jesus, speak for me, plead for me, come between my soul and my offended God, that I perish not. Amen.

To Thee, O God, the fount of mercy, I, a sinner, draw near. From my uncleanness, therefore, deign Thou to cleanse me. Enlighten my blindness, O sun of justice; bind up my wounds, O eternal physician. Thou King of kings, clothe my nakedness; lead me back, good shepherd, to the fold from which I have strayed; Thou mediator between God and man, clear away my guilt. Have pity, O God, on my misery; grant indulgence to my crimes; restore me life for death, virtue for impiety, and to my obduracy apply Thy saving grace. O Thou most clement one, call me back fleeing from Thee, draw me when resisting, raise me when I fall, support me having risen, and lead me as I walk. Do not forget me when I forget Thee, nor turn Thou away when I forsake Thee; despise me not in the midst of my sins.

By sinning I, have offended Thee, my God, I have injured my neighbor, I have wounded myself. By my weakness, O my God, have I sinned against Thee, the all wise Son; through my malice, against Thee, meek Spirit of God. Thus have I offended Thee, most excellent Trinity. Alas for my misery! How many and what great faults of divers kinds I have committed! I have abandoned Thee, O Lord; I have murmured against Thy goodness; and when confronted by base pleasure, or deterred by misfortune, I have preferred rather to lose Thee than to forego the things that allure, to offend Thee than to incur the things that I fear. O my God, how far I have gone astray in word and deed! I have sinned in secret and in public contumaciously. Hence, I beseech Thee that, because of my weakness Thou wilt not regard my iniquity, but Thine own immense goodness, and, bestowing upon me sorrow for the past and care for the future, wilt mercifully forgive what I have done.

O God, I am very sorry that I have sinned against Thee who art so good. Forgive me for Jesus' sake, and I will try to sin no more. Amen.

O God, I love Thee with my whole heart and above all things and am heartily sorry that I have offended Thee. May I never offend Thee any more. Oh, may I love Thee without ceasing, and make it my delight to do in all things Thy most holy will. Amen.

O most gracious Virgin Mary, beloved Mother of Jesus Christ my Redeemer, intercede for me with Him. Obtain for me the full remission of my sins, and perfect amendment of life, unto salvation of my soul, and the glory of His Name. Amen

I implore the same grace of thee, O my angel guardian; of you my holy patrons, N. N.; of you O holy Peter and holy Magdalen, and of all the Saints of God. Intercede for me a sinner, repenting of my sins, and resolving to confess and amend them. Amen.

O God, I love Thee with my whole heart and above all things and am heartily sorry that I have offended Thee. May I never offend Thee any more. Oh, may I love Thee without ceasing, and make it my delight to do in all things Thy most holy will. Amen.

Here may be said the Miserere (Psalm 50), or any of the Penitential Psalms.

PRAYERS AFTER CONFESSION

After Confession we should return thanks to God for His mercies in forgiving our sins, beg that He supply whatever has been wanting to us and bless our good resolutions, and immediately thereafter say our penance (if one has been given).

I thank Thee, my God, for giving me the forgiveness of my sins, through the Precious Blood of Jesus Christ my Saviour. Bless the Lord, O my soul, and all that is within me, bless His holy Name.

O most merciful God, who in forgiving our sins, rememberest them no more against us forever, accept my unworthy thanks for Thy great goodness in blotting out my transgressions. Let the grace of this absolution strengthen and sustain me, and may the pitifulness of Thy great mercy defend me evermore from all assaults of the enemy. Amen.

Now perform the penance, if the Priest has assigned one to you, as follows:

O Lord God, I desire to offer Thee the penance which Thou hast given me by the word of Thy Priest. It is nothing compared to the sins which I have committed: nevertheless, I unite it to the sufferings of my Lord and Saviour Jesus Christ and offer it as an act of adoration of Thy divine Majesty, of sorrow for my sins (especially ...), and of supplication for the virtues of...

Then say your penance.

O my God, I resolve to show my thanks to Thee for receiving me as Thy forgiven child, by fighting against sin in the future. I resolve by Thy grace to avoid what is wrong, to believe what is true, to do what is right, and to continue Thy faithful soldier and servant unto my life's end.

May the holy Mother of God, my Guardian Angel, and my holy Patrons, N.N., join with me in giving thanks unto the Lord for his great goodness, and loving kindness, in pardoning mine iniquity. And may the eternal Father, of His boundless mercy and by the life and death of His dear Son, enable me to persevere unto the end, and die in His favour. Amen.